Transgender Intersections

Transgender Intersections

Race and Gender through Identities, Interactions, and Systems of Power

CAREY JEAN SOJKA AND
KYLAN MATTIAS DE VRIES

polity

Copyright © Carey Jean Sojka & Kylan Mattias de Vries 2025

The right of Carey Jean Sojka and Kylan Mattias de Vries to be identified as Author of this Work has been asserted in accordance with the UK Copyright, Designs and Patents Act 1988.

First published in 2025 by Polity Press

Polity Press
65 Bridge Street
Cambridge CB2 1UR, UK

Polity Press
111 River Street
Hoboken, NJ 07030, USA

All rights reserved. Except for the quotation of short passages for the purpose of criticism and review, no part of this publication may be reproduced, stored in a retrieval system or transmitted, in any form or by any means, electronic, mechanical, photocopying, recording or otherwise, without the prior permission of the publisher.

ISBN-13: 978-1-5095-6015-8
ISBN-13: 978-1-5095-6016-5(pb)

A catalogue record for this book is available from the British Library.

Library of Congress Control Number: 2024948529

Typeset in 11 on 14pt Warnock Pro
by Cheshire Typesetting Ltd, Cuddington, Cheshire
Printed and bound in Great Britain by CPI Group (UK) Ltd, Croydon

The publisher has used its best endeavours to ensure that the URLs for external websites referred to in this book are correct and active at the time of going to press. However, the publisher has no responsibility for the websites and can make no guarantee that a site will remain live or that the content is or will remain appropriate.

Every effort has been made to trace all copyright holders, but if any have been overlooked the publisher will be pleased to include any necessary credits in any subsequent reprint or edition.

For further information on Polity, visit our website:
politybooks.com

Contents

1. Intersectionality and Trans Experience	1
2. Gendered Racialization	32
3. Multiraciality	54
4. Whiteness	73
5. Race and Gender Intersections with Social Class, Sexuality, Disability, and Nationality/Citizenship	98
6. Intersectional Trans Futures	117
Appendix: Methodology	139
References	146
Index	166

1

Intersectionality and Trans Experience

Lance sat across from me in a crowded coffee shop, a cool break from the humid upper Midwest weather. Wearing jeans, a casual button-up shirt, and boots, Lance was friendly and excited to share his story. A few months prior, Lance had emailed me in response to my posts to interview trans people of color, asking if he qualified for the study because, he told me, "I'm perceived as a white man now."

As a Native person, Lance had been typically assumed to be non-white when he was growing up; he was often asked the racialized question "what are you?" by others. During the interview, Lance shared about his experiences growing up in the rural Midwest, in an Indigenous family that attempted

---

This chapter is derived in part from the article "Transgender People of Color at the Center: Conceptualizing a New Intersectional Model" by Kylan Mattias de Vries, published in *Ethnicities* in 2015 © SageJournals, available online: https://doi.org/10.1177/1468796814547o. Reprinted by permission of SageJournals. This chapter is also derived in part from the article "Intersectional Identities and Conceptions of the Self: The Experience of Transgender People" by Kylan Mattias de Vries, published in *Symbolic Interaction* in 2012 © John Wiley and Sons, Inc., available online: https://www.jstor.org/stable/symbinte.35.1.49. Reprinted by permission of John Wiley and Sons, Inc.

to assimilate into white settler culture, although they went back to the reservation in the summers when he was young. Once he moved out on his own, he wanted more information about his Native heritage: "I've tried to talk to my parents about [our Native identities] more, because it is not something they shared with me growing up." His dad didn't feel comfortable in their predominantly white town, but "he would always say 'conform, conform, conform' [to white society], and that was really hard. . . ." He told me about his Native father who grew up on a reservation, his mother who is of mixed heritage, the lessons he learned from both of his parents about his and his family's identities, and the ways he has navigated these throughout his life.

However, as Lance transitioned, the gender meanings of his appearance also shifted the way others understood his race, and he started to be perceived more often as white. Lance reflected on many experiences throughout his life of moving between categories: between being perceived as a boy or a girl, a woman or a man, non-white or white, Indigenous or settler, and more. Lance shared that:

> It's like it's the two worlds that always pushes me. It's the reason why I can be an intellectual and be in graduate school and work with my hands [as a tradesperson] in another world because that's who I am. And probably, it's probably that way that my parents trained me to be two things but also the fact that I've always had these two things inside me. We were talking about gender or race. It's part of the reason I can straddle and see lots of different ways it can work. It's part of the reason why I do very well when couples break up. Because I can hear one person and then hear the other person's perspective and not be confused (laughing). To me it's all, there's always this duality. It's even more than a duality; it's sort of like this multiplicity of who people are and that's not confusing to me. It's like, of course that's how everybody works.

Intersectionality and Trans Experience 3

Fast forward sixteen years later, and we now sit across from each other on a video conferencing call. Other than some gray hairs, not much of his appearance has changed, and Lance gives off the same easy going, friendly vibes. Lance still has a strong working-class identity, and he is proud to be associated with the trades, even though he says he is now more "adjacent to the trades" because he has a leadership role working directly with tradespeople.

He tells me more about his Native identity, sharing more information about his father (Assiniboine (Nakoda)) and his mother (Cherokee and white). He talks about how his identity is complicated by his parents' shame around their Indigenous heritage, which he attributes to histories of genocidal practices, and how he's explored that more since we last talked. Lance remarked: "Because of genocide stuff, my parents were trying to act like we are white, right? . . . And it's been digging some of that up and trying to understand what happened." He also tells me that since we last talked, "I've had more contact with people in my tribe. So that's been good," and he shares that better understanding his tribal culture continues to be really important to him.

Through it all, Lance talks to me about interconnections between whiteness, settlers, Indigeneity, race, gender, and class in his life. We get on the topic of Two-Spirit identities; as Laing notes, Two-Spirit is an identity for some Indigenous people and can refer to "one's sexuality, gender, and the roles one fills in community"; however, Two-Spirit people also complicate the term, using it as "a way to refuse to give people a straight answer about themselves, their bodies, and their relationships" (2021:151). Although Lance does not identify as Two-Spirit himself, we talk about the complexity of this identity and the misunderstandings and misuse of the term. He says:

> There's a lot of white people that want to jump on this idea, which I think of as essentialism, where they're like, "we've existed

forever and look at these Two-Spirit people and blah blah blah." And I have a very hard time with that, because that's not understanding the whole picture of Two-Spirit, it's not, I mean, would all the Two-Spirit people I know call themselves trans? Probably not, right. And I think that there's a lot of misconception that that is an identity that's similar or the same as trans. And you know, it's about spirituality, it's about connection to the natural world, it's about connection to your community. And you know, there's a lot of trans identities that are not about that. I think that there's a lot of talk where people use Two-Spirit as a way to be like, "proof that we exist and we're real." I'm like oh, no, no, no, no, not on my watch, not doing that shit.

Lance's story, like that of many Indigenous trans and Two-Spirit people, challenges settler colonial understandings of gender as well as what it means to be Indigenous (binaohan 2014; Laing 2021; Pyle 2019; Rifkin 2012; Robinson 2020). Lance grew up being perceived as a girl of color most of the time, and more particularly being identified by others as Indigenous in Indigenous spaces; however, as he transitioned, he began to be recognized not just as a man, but predominantly as a non-Indigenous white man. This was based on how others perceived his changing bodily features. While he expected others' perceptions of his gender to change through transition, he was unprepared for others' perceptions of his race and Indigeneity to change through transition as well. Because of the embodied ways that gender and race are linked in how we perceive people in our society, his gender transition was also a racialized transition. Gender and race, for Lance and for other trans people, are intimately interconnected.

*　*　*

In *Transgender Intersections*, we start from the stories of trans people such as Lance, investigating relationships between gender, race, and other social categories to better understand the ways that experiences of identity intersect. We dig into why we need an intersectional approach to understand trans experience that centers race and racialization. Much political, social, and media discourse assumes a monolithic trans experience, one that too often privileges white experience. We seek to instead center an analysis of racialized gender experiences in the lives of transgender people and to use an intersectional framework to understand the complexities of people's lives.

Patricia Hill Collins defines intersectionality as the "analysis claiming that systems of race, social class, gender, sexuality, ethnicity, nation, and age form mutually constructing features of social organization, which shape Black women's experiences and, in turn, are shaped by Black women" (2000:299). Rooted in Black feminist work (Combahee River Collective 1995; Crenshaw 1991; see Collins and Bilge 2020), we explore the concept of intersectionality as it relates to transgender experience in the USA and how it helps us to consider critical questions in trans studies: How is gender racialized and how is race gendered? Why do we need an intersectional framework to understand the experiences of trans people? How are the intersecting meanings of race and gender connected to our bodies, our identities, our interpersonal interactions, and the social institutions in which we live?

Drawing on intersectional and feminist standpoint theories, *Transgender Intersections* situates trans people's experiences at the center of theorizing to offer a new perspective to the paradigm of intersectionality. Some trans people such as Lance are consciously aware of the ways that their gender – and their gender transition experiences, if they transition – are intimately connected to and shaped by race; even for those who are not aware of it, we argue that gender and race are always intersecting in the lives of trans people. These intersections impact trans people's identities, their interactions with others, and their experiences of oppression and privilege within institutions and society. In what follows, we begin by reviewing

6 Transgender Intersections

some of the scholarship of intersectionality, discussing our use of symbolic interactionism to investigate intersectionality, and framing intersectional scholarship in terms of its significance for transgender studies. Centering trans people, we will then present an intersectional model, which we use to analyze trans people's experiences in this book.

Understanding Intersectionality

The term intersectionality, coined by Crenshaw (1989), is rooted in Black feminist activism and scholarship in the USA. In the 1970s, the Combahee River Collective, a collective of Black feminists, released a foundational statement articulating their multiple marginalizations, political struggles, and the need for a new revolutionary approach to political action (Combahee River Collective 1995). This work, and other activist and scholarly contributions from women of color during this time, further inspired Black feminist scholars and activists, such as Collins (2000), Crenshaw (1989, 1991), Glenn (2002), hooks (2000), and many others, who opposed "either/or" thinking and introduced multiple oppressions/jeopardies to address the complexities of their lives. Numerous scholars have drawn on their own experiences and those of other women of color to highlight the problematic universalizing of social positions (e.g., women) within relations of power (e.g., sexism), and how women of color in the USA experience a simultaneity of racism, sexism, and classism (see Collins 1986, 2000, 2005; Crenshaw 1991; Glenn 2002; hooks 2000; May 2015; Zinn and Thornton Dill 1996; to name a few). While there are many definitions of intersectionality, Collins and Bilge present it as follows:

> Intersectionality investigates how intersecting power relations influence social relations across diverse societies as well

as individual experiences in everyday life. As an analytical tool, intersectionality views categories of race, class, gender, sexuality, [...] nation, ability, ethnicity, and age – among others – as interrelated and mutually shaping one another. Intersectionality is a way of understanding and explaining complexity in the world, in people, and in human experiences.

This working definition describes intersectionality's core insight: namely, that in a given society at a given time, power relations of race, class, and gender, for example, are not discrete and mutually exclusive entities, but rather build on each other and work together; and that, while often invisible, these intersecting power relations affect all aspects of the social world. (2020:1)

Intersectionality, then, is about simultaneously addressing lived experiences within systems of power, and examining ways to challenge and reimagine our social world.

One aspect of intersectionality relates to feminist standpoint theory (see Collins and Bilge 2020), which conceptualizes knowledge as situated and relational, rather than as objective truth (Smith 1990), what Haraway (1988) refers to as situated knowledges. Collins (2000) expands this to situate knowledge within the context of political and economic power. As such, standpoint theorists suggest that marginalized groups, who are often more aware of social positions in relation to power, serve as situated knowers (Collins 2000). The paradigm of intersectionality specifically stems from the situated knowledges of women of color in the USA. To better understand knowledge production and life experiences within the context of power, then, we should begin from the margins (hooks 2000).

Intersectionality is a complex area of theory, analysis, and praxis. Anthias notes "that 'intersectionality' does not refer to a unitary framework but a range of positions, and that essentially it is a heuristic device for understanding boundaries and hierarchies of social life" (2013:4). May also argues:

8 Transgender Intersections

> Pursuing intersectionality entails committing to a transformative collective vision and finding ways to confound and dismantle dominance by drawing on same/different logics, focusing on multiple domains of power, and attending to enmeshed identities and systems. It requires pivoting critical energies and political efforts toward unearthing suppressed complexities, contesting hidden norms and exclusions, tracing shared logics across disparate domains, and pinpointing unexpected sites of complicity or unwitting forms of collusion with dominance. (2015:251–2)

Thus, intersectionality is not just a way of better understanding the world; it is also a tool to improve it. Since it was initially introduced, a number of scholars have interrogated the methodological and theoretical aspects of intersectionality (e.g., Anthias 2013; Collins and Bilge 2020; Davis 2008; Erel et al. 2008; Lutz, Vivar, and Supik 2011; McCall 2005; May 2015; Purdie-Vaughns and Eibach 2008; Rahman 2010). Our aim is to draw from this previous work to frame an intersectional model that helps us to better understand the lives of trans people.

A primary consideration in framing an intersectional model is the extent of social positions or categories to include when creating an intersectional lens. While many scholars began with a focus on gender, race, and social class, this was quickly expanded to account for additional social positions such as the connection of gender, race, and social class with: sexuality (e.g., Bohrer 2019; Collins 2000; Nagel 2003; Taylor, Hines, and Casey 2010; Yarbro-Bejarano 1999); age (e.g., Gamson and Moon 2004; Warner and Brown 2011; Yuval-Davis 1997, 2006); disability (e.g., Ludvig 2006; Verloo 2006; Warner and Brown 2011; Yuval-Davis 2006); religion (e.g., Franks 2000; Friedman 2015); nationality (e.g., Mohanty 1991; Nagel 2003); and more. Lutz articulates fourteen dichotomous "lines of difference" – gender, sexuality, race,

Intersectionality and Trans Experience 9

ethnicity, nation/state, class, culture, ability, age, sedentariness/origin, wealth, west/the rest, religion, and stage of social development – where "social inequality, exclusion, marginalization and discrimination are articulated" (2002:67–8). Based on these collective works, we share a model based on twelve categories: race, gender, Indigeneity, ethnicity, culture, sexuality, class, age, ability, nationality, religion, and body size. This number is arbitrary, as any socially significant category that exists as a system of privilege, oppression, power, and domination in a society could be included, but we choose these as a beginning conceptualization of an intersectional model.

The second consideration is in terms of dichotomous understandings. In the USA, we have a strong tendency to conceive of race (white/other), class (middle class/poor), gender (men/women), and sexuality (heterosexual/homosexual) as binary categories exclusive of one another, where the dominant category in the supposedly dichotomous pair tends not to be interrogated and is often considered normative. Lutz notes that a binary conceptualization of these "lines of difference" limits our ability to assess "the spaces between" (2002:68). Even considering these categories as a continuum limits our understanding of their complexity. For instance, rather than conceiving of "gender" as woman–man, or feminine–masculine, it is important to interrogate the multifaceted aspects of the heuristic categories (Rahman 2009), such that woman and feminine or man and masculine do not automatically align. Scholarship on trans people of color has also called attention to the limitations of this gender binary in research and the importance of accounting for multiplicity within social positions (e.g., Bey 2022; Galarte 2021; Haritaworn 2008; Koyama 2006; Laing 2021; Peña 2010).

As noted above, the binary understanding of these categories tends to reify dominant categories. The inherent instabilities of these categories require hierarchical conceptions to maintain them, where "the dominant category is rendered 'normal' and therefore 'transparent'," or what Brekhus (1998) refers to as unmarked, and the "other" is considered deviant and problematic or marked (Glenn 2002:13). Intersectional models need to account for these unmarked categories and analyze their interconnections.

Finally, existing power structures benefit from maintaining these dichotomies and pitting them in opposition to one another. Anthias (2013) emphasizes the importance of considering social structures in the analysis of all social phenomena. Social structures, composed from various institutions in a given culture, include political, economic, military, kinship, religious, and educational dimensions; therefore, power is a key unit, especially in its effects on interaction since people rarely share equal power (Bonilla-Silva 1996; Collins 2000; Collins and Bilge 2020; McCall and Simmons 1966; May 2015; Mills 1959; Omi and Winant 1994). Social structures influence interactions and interpretations in the creation and maintenance of identities (Altheide 2000). For example, hegemonic whiteness

> provides insights into the nature of whiteness by illuminating how societies are organized based on race and how this organization sustains white supremacy. Specifically, this framework explores how racial hierarchies are sustained via dominant racial ideologies and practices. Individual and collective actors buy into these dominant racialized standards and use them to assess where other actors should be situated on the racial hierarchy and to justify the ideological and material resources that are accessible (or not) to various actors based on these valuations. This process reinforces existing racial hierarchies as actors that are better able, or more willing to achieve these racialized standards are seen as being more valuable (and thus, more deserving of resources) than actors who are not able or willing to achieve them. (Miller 2002:2)

Intersectionality and Trans Experience

Hegemonic whiteness and the categorization and hierarchy of racial groupings interconnect with the structural conceptions of class, gender, and sexuality, since who has the power to influence the process of categorization and hierarchy is crucial (Bonilla-Silva 1996; Collins 2000, 2005; Connell 1987, 2005; Connell and Messerschmidt 2005; hooks 2000; Nagel 2003; Omi and Winant 1994). This maintenance of hierarchy, power, and privilege is achieved through "[c]ultural consent, discursive centrality, institutionalization, and the marginalization or delegitimation of alternatives" (Connell and Messerschmidt 2005:846). Cultural and structural meanings significantly factor into attributed identities and what is marked versus unmarked. As noted by several scholars, including an analysis of institutional power is a key component when theorizing about intersectionality (Collins 1986, 2000; Collins and Bilge 2020; Collins et al. 1995; Grabham 2009; May 2015). Our intersectional model articulates this interconnection through a multifaceted prism with twelve intersecting social categories, each analytically developed beyond binary conceptions to address the complexity of social positions in relation to institutional and structural power.

Systems of oppression and privilege developed simultaneously in relation to the sociohistorical context of the USA and serve to provide opportunities for some and barriers for others. As Collins notes: "Because group standpoints are situated in, reflect, and help shape unjust power relations, standpoints are not static" (2000:25); thus, Collins highlights that the intersections of social positions are not homogeneous, but multifaceted. An intersectional model must be malleable to account for multiple, complex, interconnecting categories, or social positions that are not static, stable, or universal (May 2015; Rahman 2009). The experiences of trans people of color in the USA help to illuminate the institutional meanings attached to social positions, their interconnection, and the ways they are rooted in hegemonic narratives and normative expectations.

Symbolic Interactionism and Intersectionality

Symbolic interactionism is a branch of sociological social psychology – where sociology and psychology meet. Psychologists doing social psychology often investigate individuals' conceptions of self and the intrapersonal processes involved, and *"sociological social psychology tends to examine interpersonal processes, or relations between people. It emphasizes the influence of social structures such as institutions, groups, and organizations on the individual"* (Charmaz, Harris, and Irvine 2019:3, emphasis in original).

In this book, we use the sociological social psychology framework of symbolic interactionism to examine and explore the intersectional experiences of trans people. Symbolic interactionism is "a perspective that assumes that people construct selves, social worlds, and societies through interaction" (Charmaz, Harris, and Irvine 2019:5). As sociologists, we know that social contexts shape our experiences, our identities, and our relationship to institutional and structural power. Our interactions with others have a profound effect on our development, how we understand ourselves, how we come to identify, the social positions we hold, how we see ourselves in relation to our social worlds, and our experiences of power, privilege, and oppression. Like other sociologists, we still examine broader social dynamics of power, but we do so with a focus on how interpersonal processes impact and are impacted by society. In other words, we can examine "the relationship between real, living people who think, feel, and act and the social forces that shape their thoughts, emotions, and behavior" (Charmaz, Harris, and Irvine 2019:6). Through symbolic interactionism, we investigate how the construction of our identities and institutions is achieved through meaning making, interaction, and negotiation (Blumer 1969). Similar to West and Zimmerman's (1987) "doing gender" and to the analysis of how "people engaging in everyday conduct – across a spectrum from conversation and housework to interaction styles and economic behavior – are held accountable" in relation to their "presumed" social categories (Connell 2009:105), our symbolic interactionism approach helps us to identify how "the conduct produced in the light of this accountability is not a product of gender; it is gender itself" (Connell 2009:105).

In our intersectional analysis, we are interested in how that conduct is not just gender itself, but is also connected with other social categories such as race. Using symbolic interactionism to study intersectionality means addressing the ways that various hierarchical social positions or identities (around race, gender, sexuality, social class, etc.) are intimately intertwined with each other. These social positions are rooted within as well as shape institutional and structural systems of power relations, and symbolic interactionism helps us to understand the relationship between the micro and macro levels of intersectional analysis. While analyzing individuals' identities and experiences, we also address their social positions within a society and within systems of power. A key component of symbolic interactionism is the way in which meanings, in this case the meanings around intersecting social categories, are negotiated and managed within interactions. Individuals have some agency in responding within these interactions, though this agency may be constrained by the institutional and social structural power they experience with their intersecting social positions.

While at times an aspect of one's identity may seem more salient in an interaction, the other social positions one holds still factor into that interaction, regardless of whether that identity is marginalized or privileged in a society. We also follow the lead of Howard and Renfrow who argue that, in addition to the important work of addressing marginalized intersecting social positions or identities, "shining light explicitly on the privileges associated with certain social positions is important to furthering the goal of social justice" (2014:98).

14 Transgender Intersections

When addressing these intersecting social positions, we work to highlight how both marginalized and privileged positions, in intersection, all play a significant part in shaping trans people's experiences and identities.

Intersectional Trans Studies

Transgender studies has rapidly grown in the last few decades. Historically, much of the research and knowledge about trans people in the USA has been based on middle-class white trans people's experiences. In Schilt and Lagos's (2017) review of primarily sociological trans studies research in the USA, they highlight two paradigms: early research (1960–90) which focused on gender "deviance" with trans people as the objects of study, and more recent work which centers trans people as the subjects of study in examining gender difference. The last couple of decades have seen an increase in the inclusion of and/or focus on trans BIPOC experiences (e.g., Bey 2022; Chan 2018; Davis 2023; Galarte 2021; Green and Bey 2017; Heidenreich 2020; Hoston 2018; Howard et al. 2019; Hsu 2022; Krell 2017; Laing 2021; Rizki 2019; Sevelius 2013; Thai, Budge, and McCubbin 2021; Vidal-Ortiz 2009). This research suggests trans people's experiences of shifting inequality are varied and influenced by other intersecting social positions. This recent work is increasingly attentive to the intersection of social categories, addressing the ways identities, hierarchical social locations/positions (e.g., gender, race, ethnicity, social class, sexuality, nationality, age, and ability), and geopolitical place shape trans people's sense of self, experiences, and interactions with others. It also addresses important dimensions of the intersections between race and trans experience, such as historical accounts (Betancourt 2020; Ferguson 2018; Reay 2020; Snorton 2017; Zabus and Coad 2014); Black, Indigenous, and other trans people of color's experiences within communities

Intersectionality and Trans Experience 15

of color (Chen 2019; Hoston 2018); intersections between trans studies and racial and ethnic studies (Galarte 2021); Indigeneity and Two-Spirit identities (Laing 2021; Pyle 2019; Rifkin 2012; Robinson 2020); decolonizing transness (binaohan 2014; Boellstorff et al. 2014); whiteness and rurality (Abelson 2019); incarceration and the prison industrial complex (Fischer 2019; Spade 2015; Stanley and Smith 2015); citizenship and belonging (Beauchamp 2010; Haritaworn 2010); cultural productions (Chen 2019; Gossett, Stanley, and Burton 2017); children and youth (Gill-Peterson 2018); the complexity of racial and gender identities (Brubaker 2018); politics (Chaudhry 2019); migration (Josephson 2023; Luibheid and Chávez 2020); capitalism (Heidenreich 2020); and more. Intersectional analysis allows us to better understand diverse trans experiences and challenge normative social locations (e.g., white, monoracial).

The identities experienced, performed, and resisted by trans people serve as reflections of the multidimensional ways in which institutions and social systems combine and produce specific positions and facets of inequality. Social categories (e.g., race, social class, gender, etc.) intersect to inform various configurations of social relations and the social locations that groups and individuals hold in the USA. Some trans people in the USA who transition experience gender shifts in relation to hegemonic and normative cultural narratives. These dominant narratives shape the institutional meanings attached to different social positions. As such, trans people's stories and counter-narratives offer a rich analysis. Centering trans people's experiences in intersectional analysis illuminates ways individuals draw upon hegemonic and cultural constructions about social positions and the significance of these intersections to understand themselves. Furthermore, their experiences reveal how people incorporate perceptions of others' attributions of multiple social positions.

Trans people's experiences are essential to understanding racialized gender hierarchies. However, some research on trans experience has decentered trans people (Namaste 2000). Scholarship frequently focuses on what (white) trans people's experiences can tell us about (white) cisgender experience, often at trans Black, Indigenous, and other people of color's expense. In this book, our analysis of transgender intersectionality begins by bringing Black, Indigenous, and other trans people of color to the center, and we also investigate the intersectional experiences of white trans people by challenging the invisibility of whiteness. We draw on our analysis of the experiences trans people have shared in our research and make connections between their lives and experiences in order to craft an intersectional model that stems from – and centers – their experiences.

An Intersectional Model

By placing trans people at the center of theorizing, we share an intersectional model that can help to account for and analyze their intersecting experiences. This model is highly informed by existing intersectional work and utilizes heuristic categories to analyze the connections between social positions and institutional structural stratification. To better imagine this multidimensional analytical model, we use the metaphor of a prism (see Figure 1). This three-dimensional transparent prism is a regular dodecahedron with twelve faces or planes. Each plane is a social category such as gender or nationality, and within each plane are a number of analytical categories that further complicate the plane, including identity, attributed social positions, and the interconnection with broader social institutions and structures.

Each of the twelve planes offers a richer analytical tool than a dichotomy or line by moving beyond binary concepts and linking social positions within institutional and structural power. Then, importantly, these planes intersect: in a prism, one can

Intersectionality and Trans Experience 17

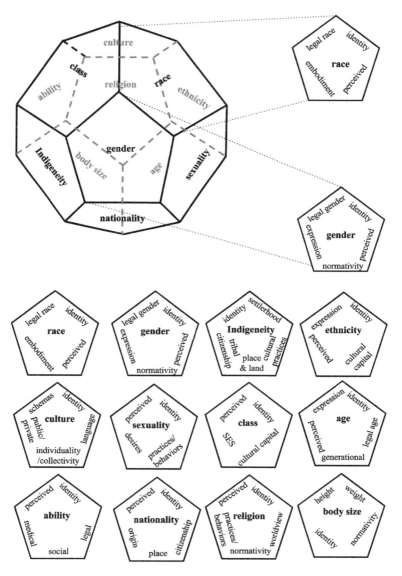

Figure 1: Multidimensional Prism

"see through" any of the planes to see the others behind or in front of it simultaneously. We can think of the space within the prism as the ways that all of the sides connect and influence each other at once. Because our aim is to address the strength of this model as intersectional, we share explanations of the planes. The foci of analysis on each plane are not meant to be limiting or exclusive of each other, but rather serve as a beginning way to conceptualize these categories and their interconnections to each other.

The category, or "plane," of race represents the many ways that racialization shapes our experiences and society. Race and racism significantly structure social experiences in the USA. The process of racialization refers to the ways racial meaning is assigned to individuals and groups through a set of social practices, and racism identifies the ways that the category of race is used in the production and maintenance of hierarchies, power, and experiences of privilege and oppression. We can analyze race along a number of different facets, including but not limited to identity, others' perceived or attributed racial categorization, legal race (how institutions categorize individuals), and meanings associated with aspects of embodiment (e.g. physical attributes). These facets may align in ways that are expected in our society, or they may also seem to contradict each other; for instance, the legal categorization of one's race may not align with how others perceive that person's race. Examining the multiple ways that race is constructed and understood in our society facilitates a more nuanced understanding not just of the category of race itself, but of the ways that race intersects with other social categories.

Gender represents many aspects of our identities, experiences, and social structures, and systems of power related to gender, such as cisgenderism and sexism, frame experiences of privilege and oppression. We can analyze gender along multiple aspects including, but not limited to, identity, gender expression, legal gender (e.g., what is indicated on a driver's license), others' perceived or attributed gender category, and the ways one aligns with or diverges from normative hegemonic gender expectations. For trans people, even the category of legal gender can be contentious. Institutional laws vary such that trans persons may be able to change their gender marker on their driver's license, but not on their birth certificate. West and Zimmerman (1987) note the way individuals engage in doing gender, but also how gender is done or attributed to others based on hegemonic and institutionalized meanings; we refer to this as "gender expression." The way individuals dress, move through the world, speak and generally interact are all assigned meanings based on social structural definitions. The planes of race and gender then intersect across many areas of our social world. In fact, they cannot be clearly separated. Experiences of race influence our experiences of gender, and vice versa. Racism is gendered, and cisgenderism (a system which privileges gender normativity) and sexism are racialized. In addition, race and gender intersect with other social planes as well.

The experiences of Indigenous peoples alongside genocidal practices, federal regulations, politics of "authenticity," and ongoing settler colonization have created contested meanings around Indigenous identity (see McKay 2021). McKay suggests incorporating Holm, Pearson, and Chavis's (2003) "peoplehood matrix" to understand Indigeneity:

> A complete system that centers and integrates the temporality, diversity, and interrelatedness of indigeneity through four aspects – language, sacred history, place territory, and ceremonial cycle. Through the lens of peoplehood, we may discover old ways and determine new ways of belonging – ways that forgo racialized objects meant to divide and exclude. (McKay 2021:23)

For this model, we have included identity (how one defines oneself); tribal relationships and/or membership; connection to land and place; cultural practices, referring to "tribal-specific traditions, knowledges, and values" (McKay 2021:13); and relationships with settler society or settlerhood (Ineese-Nash 2020) on the plane of Indigeneity. Indigeneity and nation can also have a complex relationship; many Indigenous nations may not be recognized by others as nation-states because they are actively colonized.

Another plane, ethnicity, is often intimately related to but not the same as race. Hamer et al. (2020) found significant variation in definitions of ethnicity and ethnic group across nation-states, scholars, media, and the general public. They note that the definitions are fluid, sometimes associated with nation, race, and/or culture. However, "'ethnicity' usually implies a shared identity and cultural ancestry whereas 'race' does not . . . [and] 'culture' is viewed as a broader concept" (Hamer et al. 2020:33). Ethnicity is further complicated through this intersectional model, such that the dominant group's racial categories influence ethnic identities. Ethnicity may also provide cultural capital. In the case of panethnicity, Espiritu (1992) and Nagel (1996) outline some of the political benefits of a larger group collective identity. Ethnicity can be highly connected to race and/or culture, but we separate this out as a plane of analysis in our model. Ethnicity, then, is analyzed through identity; others' perceived or attributed ethnic categorization, ethnic expression, and cultural capital. Ethnocentrism is the system of power that uses these facets of ethnicity to create and maintain social hierarchies related to belonging and cultural norms.

Culture is highly intertwined with ethnicity. In our model, culture can be analyzed along five aspects: individual identities, related to cultural belonging; cultural schemas or representations that "[convey] something meaningful about the world" (Boutyline and Soter 2021:750); language; extent of individualistic or collective cultures; and variations in the expression of culture personally and publicly. This plane conceptualizes culture as socially dynamic; people are often aware of normative cultural expectations and have agency to contest these.

Sexuality, addressing sexual and/or romantic desire or lack thereof, can include many aspects, and there are many systems of power related to hierarchies of sexuality, including heterosexism (a system which privileges heterosexuality), monosexism (a system which privileges experiences of people who sexually and/or romantically desire people of only one gender and which oppresses people who sexually and/or romantically desire people of more than one gender, such as bisexual or pansexual people), alloism (a system which privileges people who experience sexual desire and oppresses people who do not, such as asexual people), and more. Sexuality can be examined in terms of identity, perceived or attributed categorization, and one's desires and practices/behaviors; scholars often analyze sexuality in terms of identity, behavior, and desire (see Laumann et al. 1994). How others perceive someone's sexuality, or the sexual category they attribute to an individual, has a profound effect on the interaction, and the meanings others draw from are based on hegemonic cultural meanings. The intersection of bodies and our language about bodies brings more complex analyses to sexuality, sometimes related to the inadequacy of language and/or bodies and embodiment not aligning with normative expectations (see Valentine 2007). In response, trans people and their partners often negotiate and reframe language around bodies and understandings of embodiment (Chudyk 2023; Cromwell 1999; Zamantakis 2022). Moreover, sometimes participants experience new attractions. For example, Jake, an upper-middle-class African American trans man, shared that he was now unsure about his sexuality and his new fascination with gay porn, having previously been attracted to women: "I think that's where the whole fluid sexuality comes into play . . . Is it because I'm fascinated with the male body because it's what I want to have, or is it because there's something else?" In this sense, Jake was unsure if his desire for a particular masculine embodiment was related to how he envisioned himself, or an actual attraction to men. A strength of this model is the multifaceted plane of sexuality that allows us to analyze a complexity of identity, desires, and behaviors.

The category of class refers to many aspects related to wealth, income, and socialization processes related to class status, and classism is a significant structuring system in a capitalist society. Social class may be considered along four aspects of analysis: one's identity, perceived or attributed social class by others, socioeconomic status (SES), and cultural capital. For example, the contemporary working class in the USA includes those who typically obtain a high school education, often with some college or vocational education, earn over the minimum wage, and in healthy economies live above the poverty line (Erdmans 2004). In contrast, middle-class individuals tend to receive higher education, work in professional fields and hold greater power – "economic power, political power (supervising the behavior of workers), and ideological power (defining the meaning of behavior, e.g., labeling manual work as undesirable)" (Erdmans 2004:53). This provides middle-class people with more social or cultural capital – language skills, cultural competence, knowledge – which they pass down to the next generation, giving them greater rewards and opportunities.

Age is considered along the planes of legal age, perceived age, one's identity and group connectedness, expression in terms of social contexts, and generational ties. The strength of identifying with a particular age group in this research seemed to oscillate between those under the age of twenty-one (e.g., who could not access bar culture) and those over about fifty-five (thinking about end-of-life plans). In addition, in an interview with Amber (a fourth generation American Chinese trans woman), she indicated that generational context mattered especially for some Asian Americans.

Ableism is a system of power that frames the oppression of disabled people in our social world. Ability is analyzed in terms of one's identity; perceived or attributed disability; as well as definitions of disability that are represented by external systems, such as medical and legal systems. Medical and legal definitions of disability are often highly gatekeeping and otherwise problematic (see Kafer 2013 for a discussion of the medical model). However, the reality of disabled life means that experiences of disability can be shaped by these systems. For instance, having a non-apparent disability leads to different interactions than having a disability that is apparent to others, and having a disability that is legally recognized or medically diagnosed can lead to different experiences than having a disability that is not legally or medically validated.

Nationalism frames understandings of belonging and exclusion, defining an idealized citizen within a nation-state. Nationality is analyzed in terms of one's identity, perceived nationality, citizenship (as this may or may not be linked to nationality), origin (thinking about increasing global movement and where one might have a sense of belonging), and place or location. This could be further complicated with a consideration of nationality in relation to geopolitics, diasporas, and thinking about the Global North, the Global South, and Müller's call for consideration of the Global East: "Thinking with the East means drawing out the silences of the hemispheric North–South divisions, working not so much from its margins as from its interstices. The idea is not to resurrect another binary – that of West–East – but to destabilise the binary geopolitical imagination through the introduction of a *tertium quid*" (2020:749, emphasis in original).

Religion is yet another social category of importance in intersectionality. Religion can be analyzed in terms of one's identity; perceived religious affiliation; sense of practices and behaviors; worldview, or how a religious belief system shapes a believer's worldview; and what religion and practices are normative for a given society. For instance, Joshi outlines how the ethos of Christian normativity in the USA makes Christian values intrinsic to our national identity, conveys the status of truth and rightness on Christian culture, and makes Christian language and metaphors and their underlying theology the national standard. Christian normativity imbues Christianity with a unique power, situating it as ordinary and expected. As a result, atheists and religious minorities who embrace different practices, belief systems, and world views are disadvantaged relative to their Christian peers. Very real everyday consequences result from a situation in which the Christian way of doing something comes to be understood as the normal way of living. (2021:3)

Body size is also a sociologically significant category. Body size can be analyzed around a number of factors including weight, height, identity in relation to embodiment (e.g. identifying as fat, plus-size, average, thin, etc.), and normative cultural meanings around particular embodiments. Body size intersects with many other social categories. For instance, White (2014:5) examines the relationship between fatness and transness, showing how these categories intersect with each other, particularly through an analysis of "fatness and gender legibility," or the somewhat ambiguous ways that the "presence/absence and location of fat plays a role in producing a successful or desired gender presentation." Sizeism reflects the privileging of particular body sizes and types over others.

The prism we present has twelve sides, but as we mentioned before, the number is arbitrary. We can add as many sides as there are sociologically significant categories that research demonstrates relate to privilege, oppression, and power. For example, we could also add a side for social hierarchies related to perceived attractiveness, which, while somewhat difficult to analyze sociologically, has been shown to relate to life outcomes on a broad social level (Monk, Esposito, and Lee 2020). Perceptions of social attractiveness, as well as oppression or privilege related to social attractiveness, can be highly influenced by other social categories. Holla and Kuipers highlight various sociological studies showing that good looks, or aesthetic capital, serve as a form of social capital:

> While all tastes involve a sensorial experience in response to specific objects or persons, the judgment of physical appearance is dually embodied: beauty standards also apply to the self and to one's own face and body. Consequently, embodied attributes like gender, sexuality and age are particularly significant in shaping and evaluating aesthetic capital, compared to, for example, judgments of paintings or books. (2016:300)

Caste is another example of a plane that could be added to the model. As Gundemeda notes: "Though caste and race are ascribed social markers, unlike race determined by colour and coloured ideologies, caste is governed by social, cultural, religious and economic factors" (2020:89). The social category of caste is one that may be more relevant in some contexts external to the USA; for instance, as Gundemeda notes, "the forms and practices of the caste system in both public and private spheres in India" continue to be relevant to people's lives (2020:106–7). While caste was not particularly significant for the contexts and participants in this research, it can be a very important plane of intersectional analysis.

Overall, there may be times and places where there are more categories that are sociologically relevant, and others where certain categories become less sociologically relevant. This fluidity of the model allows us to shift our analyses of intersectionality depending on the social context. Each side of the prism helps us understand an important aspect of a social world. Taken together, this multifaceted prism helps us to further complicate social positions, demonstrating that one's experience of gender, for example, is informed by a number of factors both within the category of gender as well as in connection with other categories. The prism is transparent, emphasizing the ways each plane influences other social positions. A particular analysis may focus on gender, yet other social positions can be "seen through" the plane of gender, and are thus relevant and influential in a full understanding of the multiple facets of gender. We can turn the gender side of the prism towards us to focus on it in more detail, but each of the other sides is always still visible in relation to gender, shaping the analysis. In addition to intersecting identities, the model attends to the ways in which social positions are informed by, and located within, structural power and hierarchies, and the potential effects of individual/collective identities that resist imposed social positions.

People use markers in interaction based on meanings from broader institutions and social structures to ascribe interconnecting social positions to others along all of the prism planes. Based on hegemonic narratives and normative expectations, individuals may be unaware of attributing normative positions to others, such as whiteness or able-bodiedness; however, these intersecting normative positions are just as important as the attribution of marginalized positions. For instance:

> The mannerisms that help define gender – the way in which people walk, swing their hips, gesture with their hands, move their mouths and eyes as they talk, take up space with their bodies – are all based upon how nondisabled people move. A woman who walks with crutches does not walk like a "woman"; a man who uses a wheelchair and a ventilator does not move like a "man." The construction of gender depends not only upon the male body and female body, but also on the nondisabled body. (Clare 1999:12)

Anthias offers a constructive critique, noting some of the problems with intersectional analysis, such as the "listing" of differences (often reduced to identities) that intersect and the impossibility of attending analytically to this plurality, as well as potential competing claims about which are the most important of these, or how many differences should be incorporated. (2013:5–6)

We may not be able to account for all sociologically relevant planes, or sides of the prism, in any particular analysis; however, the transparency of the prism exists to highlight normative positions and structures rather than to contribute to their unmarking. This multifaceted prism aims to illustrate the interconnectedness of social categories, complicate each plane of analysis, highlight normative positions (e.g., ability or whiteness) in addition to marginalized or oppressed positions, rather than universalize the experience of those who are attributed or occupy these positions, and emphasize the interconnection of social positions with broader institutions and structures.

Applying the Intersectional Model

We can use this model to understand the experiences of trans people, including some of the experiences of Lance. For instance, we can think about intersections between Indigeneity and gender for Lance to better understand how gender expectations are based in settler colonial norms (Laing 2021). The particular oppressions that trans people face in a USA context are in relation to settler colonialism. Lance's story informs us of the importance of a decolonial perspective when creating an intersectional model. His experiences of gender are greatly shaped by his Native identity as well as settler colonial contexts, and his understandings of his Native identity, as well as how others perceive or do not perceive his Indigeneity, are greatly shaped by his gender.

The planes of race and gender also significantly intersect in Lance's life. This is most apparent in his experience of being perceived more and more as a white person while others' perceptions of his gender changed through his transition. His experience demonstrates how the process of racialization, of others attributing a racial identity or how someone is perceived racially, is intimately interconnected with gender attribution. Lance shared: "race is a construction 'cause if you can look at me and tell me I'm completely white, well that's interesting, because you constructed for yourself what white looks like." The meanings others attach to his new masculine identity are rooted in white normativity. Ward defines white normativity as the "cultural norms and practices that make whiteness appear natural, normal, and right" (2008:564); she emphasizes that this systematically supports other normative expectations such as middle-class status and heterosexuality. Lance continues to explain:

> When I was a kid I'd always have people ask me, "What are you?" They'd look at me and think I was Asian, which is pretty common. People often think that Native Americans are Asian, because of our eyes and stuff like that . . . And it's been interesting in the transition, 'cause my facial structure has changed so much that I don't get that question as often as I use to. 'Cause my cheek bones don't look the same, my face has gotten whiter.

For Lance, becoming a man is intimately connected to learning what it means to be white and heterosexual, because these are the assumptions others now place upon him. In addition, this white heterosexual masculine attribution came with a racialized gender advantage in "the form of authority, reward, and respect" (Schilt 2006:483).

We can also use the model to think about how categories such as disability are related to gender, class, and others.

Intersectionality and Trans Experience 29

When I first interviewed Lance, he was able-bodied, and when I interviewed him again, he had since developed a disability. Lance found a different, more accommodating type of employment that was also closely tied to his identity as a working-class tradesperson. Lance resisted an identity of disabled in relation to his experience, and he also shared his concern about collapsing transness and disability onto each other. Lance opposed the ways some have labeled transgender as a psychological disability, and how to be understood authentically by various social institutions (e.g., to change a legal gender marker) can mean aligning oneself with that framing. This social discourse around transness and disability influenced his own identities; Lance then resisted an identity as disabled in relation to the disability he had developed in part because of this.

We can further consider how the planes of class intersect with race, ability, and gender. Lance's association with the trades was in relation to the cultural capital he had both accumulated and continued to take part in; he had credibility with those he worked with. In addition, being perceived as a white, working-class, able-bodied man shaped opportunities for him to disrupt this attribution and challenge the cultural schemas those interacting with him relied on. This attributed normative identity created spaces where others felt they could make sexist, racist, ableist, or other problematic comments to Lance, which in turn provided him with a venue to challenge them. Lance utilized his working-class cultural capital to educate those he worked with, who were then more likely to pay attention to what he was saying and consider it relevant and authentic.

Lance's experiences help to illustrate the ways this multifaceted model is fluid instead of static. The interactions individuals experience may vary by context and across time. What identities or social positions are attributed to Lance, for example, depend on the social positions and identities others

30   Transgender Intersections

hold, the situation this is occurring in, and how well others know Lance.

Transgender Intersectionality

In *Transgender Intersections*, we will explore various aspects of intersections between race, gender, and other social categories through the lives of trans people. We build upon our intersectional model that links multifaceted social positions to institutional and structural inequalities, challenges binary divisions, and brings marginalized groups to the center of analysis by centering transgender lives. Across this book, we draw on our analysis of four data sets: two with trans people of color; one with predominantly white, rural trans people as well as some BIPOC rural trans people and a few rural partners and parents of trans people; and one with the partners of trans people (see the Appendix for details).

In Chapter 2, we further address the concept of gendered racialization, investigating intersections between gender and race in the lives of transgender people of color. We draw on the stories of trans people of color to analyze the importance of intersectionality to understanding trans experience more broadly. We examine intersections of gender and race for trans people of color in relation to both BIPOC communities and broader systems of settler white supremacy. We will also address how these intersections shape social visibility for trans people of color.

In Chapter 3, we analyze the experiences of six multiracial trans people who shared their stories with us to examine the boundaries between racial categories as they intersect with gender. These research participants experienced shifts in how others perceived their race; for these six people, racial boundaries are influenced by, and influence, gender perceptions. While this is true for all people, the changing perceptions of both gender and racial categories for these multiracial trans people somewhat uniquely emphasize aspects of intersectionality that may otherwise go unnoticed.

We turn in Chapter 4 to an analysis of the dominant racial category, whiteness, as well as settler colonialism. We analyze trans people of color's understandings of whiteness, and we draw from interviews with white trans people to investigate the intersections between race and gender in relation to whiteness, white normativity, and white supremacy in more detail. We also examine trans people's relationships to settler colonialism.

While we bring in analysis related to more than only gender and race in the previous chapters, in Chapter 5 we further explore an intersectional approach to understanding trans lives. We move deeper into some additional social categories, including social class, sexuality, disability, and nationality and citizenship, with examples from trans people's experiences that help us to understand these other planes of intersectionality.

We end in Chapter 6 by addressing the political climate of transgender intersectionality in the USA today. We highlight trans people's analyses of our social world and their concern about anti-trans, white supremacist, and other oppressive social contexts. We also share the ways that the trans people we have interviewed are imagining and building intersectional trans futures, highlighting ideas for creating a more just world.

2

Gendered Racialization

Josie and Katrice asked if they could do their interviews together and also take me on a tour of where they lived. Over the course of several hours, in two coffee shops as well as driving around their southern town, Josie and Katrice shared their experiences as Black trans women. Katrice talked about trying to join a trans peer support group in search of community and resources when she was first transitioning. White people in the group deliberately and repeatedly told her the wrong days and times for meetings so she could not attend, and they refused to share resources about medical and behavioral health providers who worked with trans people. Because of experiences like this, of exclusion from white-dominated

---

This chapter is derived in part from the article "Intersectional Identities and Conceptions of the Self: The Experience of Transgender People" by Kylan Mattias de Vries, published in *Symbolic Interaction* in 2012 © John Wiley and Sons, Inc, available online: https://www.jstor.org/stable/symbinte.35.1.49. Reprinted by permission of John Wiley and Sons, Inc. This chapter is also derived in part from the article "Transgender People of Color at the Center: Conceptualizing a New Intersectional Model" by Kylan Mattias de Vries, published in *Ethnicities* in 2015 © SageJournals, available online: https://doi.org/10.1177/14687968145470. Reprinted by permission of SageJournals.

trans community spaces, both Katrice and Josie shared how their activism was shaped by needing "to get our house together" first; their primary goal was to support other Black trans people in their work, and they built on lessons they had learned from civil rights activists in their families of origin in doing this. For them and for other Black, Indigenous, and other trans people of color from this research, race is and needs to be central in trans liberation.

Gendered Racial and Ethnic Expectations

The process of developing a sense of self not only involves individuals' self-concepts, but also others' perceptions of them and whether or not these align. In the case of transgender people, their gender self-concept may not match what others assign to them; thus, others' confirmation of one's gender identity can be a powerful force. For many trans people who make use of hormones and/or surgeries, the resulting changes in embodiment can significantly impact how others perceive them. In these situations, a trans person who transitions may experience aspects of gender socialization because of new types of gendered interactions and experiences with others. This socialization can also include learning the various ways that race, social class, sexuality, and other social categories, in intersection with gender, inform the meanings others draw upon in relation to their gender presentation. The planes of race, class, gender, sexuality, and more combine in specific ways such that others attribute these various combinations to trans people in interaction, therefore influencing how trans people see themselves. This can unexpectedly complicate people's self-perceptions through transition. Drawing on ethnographic data primarily with Black, Indigenous, and other trans people of color, we analyze the intersected identity frames, or the ways that race, social class, gender, and

34   Transgender Intersections

sexuality all intersect to create specific background identities that others attribute to individuals to frame their interaction (Goffman 1974). We can better understand these intersected identity frames through the experiences of trans people who engage in identity management. The meanings others attach to specific combinations are foregrounded in the context of transitioning, and these interactions take place in a larger context as well; some interactions occur with others who employ dominant, white settler cultural narratives, while other audiences draw upon racial and ethnic cultural narratives.

Transitioning can throw the multi-dimensionality of enacted identity into sharp relief against the background of intersecting social and cultural structural arrangements. This intersectional analysis illustrates the complexity of these frames, the resourcefulness of social actors, and how these frames are enacted in social interaction. Most BIPOC participants felt it vital to learn the specific racial and ethnic cultural expectations and meanings that others attached to their new social location, particularly the intersected identity frames others would attribute within certain racial/ethnic groups/communities and how social class and sexuality intersect with these understandings.

Amber (a middle-class fourth generation Chinese American bisexual trans woman) addressed her concerns about cultural differences within Asian, Asian American, and Pacific Islander (AAPI) communities, how familial expectations were a major issue, and the notion that "rebelling against your culture or community" is not an option. Scholarship on the experiences of AAPI trans people remains lacking, and we build on the more recent work of Thai et al. (2021) and Hsu (2022). For Amber, what qualified as "rebelling" changed upon transitioning. Each racial and ethnic culture defines its members by specific intersected identity frames, so for trans people this can entail learning to negotiate multiple dimensions of what people now expect. Furthermore, the type of intersected identity frame others applied to them in specific cultural groups occasionally differed from those in dominant white settler culture, so learning about these differences, when to expect them, and how to respond to such different attributions was important in legitimizing one's gender. In this chapter, we highlight trans BIPOC experiences in relation to cultural narratives about intersected identity frames as well as social visibility related to gendered racialization.

Gendered Racialization Expectations and Interactions in BIPOC Communities

Interestingly, most of the Black trans women in this study stated they were "moving up in the African American community" (Josie, a middle-class African American trans woman). They shared their experience of being taken more seriously in the Black community. After hearing this, we asked the Black trans men if they experienced the opposite in Black communities. They uniformly replied that they did not experience a loss of status or rank (later we address how this experience differed within white dominant culture). This may be due to a few factors: first, the Black trans women in this study were older and transitioned on average nine years prior to their interview, while the Black trans men were newer to transitioning. Second, the Black trans women all identified as middle class, and their economic resources likely factored into their experiences. Third, upon transitioning, the Black trans women gained access to and participated in "women-only" spaces (e.g., beauty parlors). In general, access to and participation in specific culturally gendered spaces often conveyed others' acceptance of their racialized gender.

In addition to access to spaces, several trans men who had been active in women's communities prior to transitioning experienced a sense of loss of access to women's spaces, although they did express feeling a need to "let it go." This sense of loss is often in relation to trans men occupying a former lesbian or queer identity and being denied access to women's spaces upon transitioning.

Culturally gendered expectations also factor into "loss" of women's spaces. Several Latino trans men felt conflicting emotions over the change in gender roles within their community and, more specifically, within their families. For instance, Jacobo (middle-class Latino trans man) shared: "In the Latino community, at dinner, it's the woman that serves the food, it's the woman that prepares the food, it's the woman that cleans up the dishes." Both Jacobo and Dexter indicated that when they made efforts to help out in the kitchen, they were told by the men, "You don't have to anymore," and by women, "You don't belong in the kitchen anymore." This change in access to space also involves respecting women's spaces: "If a bunch of women are sitting around talking, you don't go over to the area and sit down" (Jacobo). While these cultural narratives were affirming in some ways, Jacobo and Dexter also found them to be limiting in terms of constructing and managing a type of masculinity they wanted for themselves.

Becoming a man of color can entail specific types of interactions with other men of color. Diego (a working-class Puerto Rican and Brown/white multiracial trans man) experienced being called "cousin" or "brother" (see Laing 2017; Majors and Billson 1992), while Jake (an upper-middle-class African American man) learned to interact in specific ways with other Black men:

> In the African American community, there's this whole other ritual of how you breathe, how you do that chest thing when you grab hands and sort of come together, and sort of stay, and then move in, so that's another thing, another layer that I now have to master.

This is similar for Jacobo in the Latinx[2] community. The racial/ethnic meanings others attach to their gender are significant and often vary from dominant, white cultural expectations. Jacobo explained how other Latinos treat him now: "They give you your place as another male Latino. They wouldn't do that to another female." Similar to ethnically gendered expectations, others employ and challenge dominant cultural narratives around intersected identity frames.

Partners of trans people also reflected on their experiences in BIPOC spaces and communities. Lola, a Black pansexual cis woman partner of David, a Black trans man, shared her perceptions of her and her partner's experiences in Black community:

> When you see him, you see a Black man. And to be around a Black community of people who understand the Black man struggle is really . . . it's important, but to be excluded from those spaces, or discounted [because of gender] is really . . . is really tough. So, it's almost like [coming] off as a heterosexual couple helps, but I hate it.

Janice, a Black queer cis femme partner of Trevor, a Black trans man, shared her experiences within queer communities as well. She noted that "even within, sort of, queer Black community, we're ostracized, too . . . Like, so it's to be an outsider within communities that we should be insiders with, in spite of the fact that people want to pretend that we're in it." She later continued, saying that her and her partner experienced "not fitting for a variety of reasons, not just race, not just gender, but, like, all of them." In these specific situations, while Lola

---

[2] Latinx and Latine, as social categories, can both be inclusive of a broad range of gender identities in discussing an ethnic and sometimes racialized experience and identity as it is shaped by dominant culture (Chavez-Dueñas et al. 2019; for a nuanced discussion of the terms Latino/a/x/e, see Miranda, Perez-Brumer, and Charlton 2023).

38   Transgender Intersections

and David's as well as Janice and Trevor's racialized gender presentations were not changing, the intersected identity frames others attributed to them were different based on the normative expectations within their communities.

Gendered Racialization and Settler White Supremacy

The meanings and types of femininities, masculinities, and other genders attributed by others to trans people vary by cultural group, social class, and regional location. Connell (1987) argues that femininities and masculinities are not fixed or linear; they are concurrently a product and producer of history. This is not to imply that each culture holds only one type of femininity and masculinity. In all cultures there are a set of hierarchies which are influenced by other social factors. Within a given culture, an emphasized femininity and hegemonic masculinity are at the top of the hierarchy and set the standards to which all other femininities and masculinities are compared (Collins 2000; Connell 1987; Schippers 2007). Thus, only a distinct minority qualifies as "truly" feminine or masculine; in the USA, this is defined as white settler, middle class, heterosexual, and in contrast to all "others" (Connell 1987; Goffman 1963). Both Josie and Katrice discussed how their exclusion from white trans spaces was in relation to antiblackness – their racialized gender did not fit the emphasized white normative femininity.

Many trans men spoke about their first time being exposed to the sexualization of women during conversations with other men. The sexualization of women can be an important part of men's homosocial spaces (Johanssen 2021; Pascoe 2005; Sanday 1990); however, how this is performed and the meanings associated with an individual's intersected identity frame vary by culture. For example, Bennyboy (working-class baklâ trans man) reflected on the following story about the cultural difference in the sexualization of women:

The other day . . . I was just sitting back actually watching [a conversation between workers on the job site]. It was sort of forty to sixty, forty being Brown and sixty being white . . . some of the Mexican guys were talking about seeing a woman, and he's like, "oh yeah my tongue got hard, you know, I saw her and my tongue got hard." . . . They always talk about going down on women and I would watch the white guys in the group and they would get super uncomfortable, and it was all about making her cum . . . versus like white guys talking about, . . . "I got this girl to go down on me, you know I don't do shit for her." . . . It's all about . . . like for Brown people being a man is more about how well you can please your partner versus how much you can get from them and not return it.

Cromwell (1999) and Rubin (2003) find that some trans men perpetuate sexist behavior as a way of enacting masculinity. While this may be the case, the type of sexism and objectification of women that some trans men participate in may differ culturally as Bennyboy states here. Additionally, several participants shared their first encounters with this sexist homosocial behavior, their discomfort with this, and concern that their silence contributed to the interaction. Similar to Dozier (2005), Schilt (2006), and Abelson's (2016b) findings, some participants shared their desire to speak out against sexism, and how this involved active engagement with their masculine narrative.

In addition to the experiences above, participants often discussed shifts in gendered racialization and systems of power through their experiences with employment. Over half of the trans men of color expressed concern about finding future employment through or after transition; all of those who did so were working class. Trent addressed his concern about job opportunities as a Black man versus when he had been perceived as a woman:

> It worries me sometimes when I think about becoming male, Black male . . . especially as I go out and . . . get a different job . . . I noticed . . . in the three different companies I worked for, especially in the career that I have, there's very few if not any people of color . . . and absolutely no Black males anywhere, in any company I worked, at the executive level, management level, or at this level or the field I'm in, and I wonder sometimes how that's going to be now that I'm going to be approaching that from a different gender now.

Trent's experience is reflective of white normative expectations in the workplace, which define who is deemed an appropriate worker through whiteness. This also highlights how anti-blackness as a form of racism shapes the cissexism and genderism experienced by Black trans people (Bey 2022; Chaudhry 2019; Green and Bey 2017; Hoston 2018; Krell 2017; Snorton 2017; Sumerau and Grollman 2020; Tinsley and Richardson 2014). At the time of the interview, Trent was considering relocating to another region of the USA to be with his partner, which would also allow him to start fresh in his masculine gender identity. In speaking with Trent two years after his initial interview, he indicated he did relocate and still was unable to find work. He felt strongly that this was a result of him "being a Black man now." In addition, although Trent was able to change his identification and found previous co-workers to provide references using his correct name and pronouns, the documentation of his gender change never truly disappeared.

The four middle- and upper-middle-class Black, Indigenous, and other trans men of color felt secure in their employment and future opportunities. In this respect, occupying a higher social class situationally muted the stigmatized position experienced by the other trans men of color. For example, Jake, an upper-middle-class Black trans man, believed his white co-workers perceived him as "being one of the good Black people." In the workplace, his upper-middle-class status, higher education, and clothing, in combination with his cultural capital, contributed to white people perceiving him as "safe" to be around; in other words, his masculine presentation was in greater alignment with hegemonic middle-class settler white heterosexual masculinity, embodied attributes that bring with them greater cultural, political, and economic rewards. The Fortune 500 company employing Jake worked with him as he transitioned, which facilitated his relationships with co-workers. These contributed to his social capital and improved his chances of mobility within the company.

The five Asian American trans women interviewed were currently or had been employed in technology fields. When they had been perceived as Asian American men prior to transition, they were often stigmatized as "nerdy," "geeky," and "smart"; these institutionalized meanings aligned with their employment in technical fields. Upon transitioning, four shared experiencing a change in their status at work and the meanings others applied to these social positions. These changes took the form of hypersexualization and/or a decrease in status. Moving from social invisibility, Miranda, Amber, and Nici felt that often white, straight cis men treated them as "a provocative sex object" (Nici, a middle-class Chinese American trans woman). Amber highlights how institutional stereotypes linking Asians with technological fields change depending on gender status: "I'm generally considered dumber. I'm the architect of the new software system and [company] that I'm starting, and have to constantly explain to people that I actually do know very much what I'm talking about." Institutionalized meanings attributed by others, and used to define employment opportunities, are intersectionally rooted in the connections between and among social categories and the intersected identity frames attributed to trans people.

Although emphasized femininity and hegemonic masculinity are currently sociopolitically defined as white settler, middle

42   Transgender Intersections

class, and heterosexual, this definition is also fluid (Connell 2005). Within dominant white culture, there are numerous femininities, masculinities, and other genders often revolving around the conceptions of race/ethnicity, class, sexuality, and more (see Charlebois 2012; Moore 2006; Schippers 2007). A key component for trans people often includes learning these numerous gender expectations, the circumstances in which others attribute these to them, and the ways to negotiate, integrate, and/or resist them.

Visibility and the Intersectionality of Gendered Racialization

Gendered racialization thus greatly influences how one is perceived as well as how one is oppressed and/or privileged in society. Within a white supremacist society, whiteness is framed as normative, and racial experiences that are not white are marked as other. This may often involve other racial categories being marked as either "too much" or "not enough" in relation to whiteness. Gendered racialization for non-white people is often marked in these ways. One area where we find this is in relation to visibility: as compared to white gender norms, Black, Indigenous, and other people of color may often experience social invisibility or social hypervisibility (and sometimes, aspects of both) in relation to white people.

Becoming Less Visible

Chou and Feagin describe Asian Americans' experience of "social invisibility" – "being ignored or not seen" (2008:65). In terms of dominant culture, specific intersected identity frames are more socially visible than others, depending not only on changes in power or status, but also on how others perceive a person as dangerous or exoticized. Chou and Feagin (2008) and Han (2009) demonstrate the ways Asian American men are feminized, emasculated, and portrayed as harmless. Dante (an upper-middle-class South Asian trans guy) felt that his transition went "smoothly." He wanted to become "a gentle guy" and reflected on how he was not stigmatized like other trans men of color. Because Asian American men are sometimes marked by others as less threatening than other men (for the most part), they become less socially visible. For Dante, his class status and college education further confirmed for others that he was "smart," "nerdy," and "safe."

Perceived femininity and "submissiveness" of Asians is illustrated by a comment from a white trans woman to Elle (a Chinese American queer trans woman), who recounted the story to me:

> Another t[ransgender] friend of mine, who transitioned at the same time as me . . . she's white or Caucasian, and one of the biggest beefs she keeps giving me is, "You're Asian, that sucks, shut up, what do you have to complain about?" 'Cause the general rule of thumb is that most Asians have an easier time transitioning.

Elle's white friend perceived Asian American trans women as having an easier time being accepted as women by others, because her assumption was that Asian American men were already perceived as feminine.

Media representations of Black men oscillate between the nonthreatening Black "buddy" and the sexually deviant and/or violent man (Collins 2005). Representations of Black women oscillate between their being considered "less" beautiful when they do not align with the standards of white middle-class femininity, and being targeted as hypersexual (Collins 2005). The Black trans women in this study moved from high stigmatization when they had been perceived as Black men to lower social visibility as Black women. This may be because most of the Black trans women we interviewed were middle-aged and that factored into the extent of social invisibility. The younger Black trans women we met at conferences expressed feeling more sexualized and that they were seen as more "exotic."

Becoming More Visible

Changes in attributed intersected identity frames also result in some trans people gaining social visibility. For many trans women, an increase in social visibility was often related to being exoticized and sexualized. For many trans men, an increase in visibility was often related to others' perceptions of them as exotic, threatening, and/or criminal.

Several scholars address the historical ways women of color have been and are hypersexualized and exoticized (Collins 2005; Nagel 2003; Wilkins 2004); this scholarship highlights the ways that hypersexualization (and desexualization) are intersectional racialized gender processes. Azhar et al. (2021) found that Asian American and Pacific Islander women continue to experience hypersexualization in the USA. The Asian American trans women in particular identified being treated as "a provocative sex object" by white men (Nici). Amber was concerned about moving from a socially invisible category (being perceived as an Asian American man) to being an Asian American woman: "now that you are a sought after item, so instead of trying to get into groups, you're trying to get away from them, like standing on a street corner [waiting for a taxi] is actually a really dangerous thing." The potential for violence against Asian American trans women is tied to white supremacist settler colonial histories that leave so-called exotic bodies more open to violence from white people. Other factors are also linked to sexualization, including age, body size, and expression of femininity. Most of the Asian American trans women maintained middle- to upper-middle-class status and their perceived femininity marked them as heterosexual. Miranda (first generation Korean trans woman) gives an example of the hypersexualization in being an Asian American woman: "I was at [company] . . . it was rumored that I was pregnant with a co-worker's baby . . . I used to swear that I'm not pregnant; I would be the first one in shock if I was." Miranda felt the rumor started because of the "strange" Asian foods she ate (supposedly an indication of pregnancy food cravings), but also that the sexualization of Asian American women contributed to co-workers insisting on her "affair."

Although Asian trans men often move to a less socially visible category, other trans men of color discussed becoming more visible. In this case, while the feminization of Asian American men (Han 2009) decreased their social visibility, the hypersexualized masculinity attributed to Black and Latino men increased their social visibility. In some instances, this increase in visibility is connected to gaining what Schilt (2006) refers to as "gender advantage," which is particularly relevant for white trans men; however, the extent of gender advantage varies by race, social class, height, and other social categories (Abelson 2019; Schilt 2006).

Collins (2005) and Nagel (2003) outline the hypersexualization of men of color and the historical representations of them as sexually dangerous, especially to white women. Scout (mixed-race trans man) explained: "I never thought about being an interracial couple before. When I was with [white girlfriend] I would get looks . . . like, 'Why are you dating a white girl?' When it wasn't a problem [before transitioning] because everyone [perceived] me as white." In some cases, the hypersexualization of some Black, Indigenous, and other men of color involves representations of them as perpetrators; in other cases, hypersexuality is exoticized, such as Dexter's experience in being perceived as a "Latin lover" (see Rodríguez 1997; Vargas 2010). Dexter perceived his hypersexualization as less dangerous, for instance, than for the Asian American trans women, but it was still disconcerting, particularly when he felt boxed into that role with partners. Dexter's approach to this new sexualization was playful; he spoke of having fun with this new intersecting identity frame by going to gay bars and playing on this "exoticizing of Latinoness." Although Dexter makes light of his experiences, he is still concerned with how this hypersexualization will influence future relationships and the potential for negative consequences when others perceive him as a threat.

Collins (2005) finds working-class Black men are more often portrayed in the media as perpetrators. As they began to transition, several Black trans men expressed concerns about now being acknowledged by others as Black men because of the type of intersecting identity frame now attributed to them: "I know that there's a stigma [that] white America has of Black men" (Trent, working-class Black trans man). Jake shared:

> When I transitioned from being an African American woman, you know that's a double minority, to being an African American man, you're probably the scariest person in the United States of America. When I walk down the street, people walk to the other side so they don't have to be near me. When I walk through the mall they follow me around and make sure I'm not stealing anything.

For Jake, his gain in gender advantage (moving from a "double minority" to a single subordinate position) was situationally muted by acquiring a more visibly stigmatized status as a Black man. Similarly, Lance (Assiniboine (Nakoda) working-class trans man) questioned: "It's like if you're female and you're seen as a person of color, what does that mean? Versus if you're seen as a man and a person of color? And what's less threatening?" The increase in social visibility is related to dominant, white racist cultural narratives that others draw upon to assign specific intersected identity frames in interaction.

Gendered Racialization

Alejandro (working-class Latino trans man) provided an illustration of a specific heteronormative, working-class intersected identity frame related to the perception of men of color as "threatening":

> I find that people are scared of me; they see a dark eyed/haired non-Anglo man walking near them off the train at night and they are scared. I am more scared of police who are always stopping me in my car. I am scared when I go to clubs and things get heavy; I have been in [three] fights. Being a Latino blue collar male, I am seen as a trouble maker, and I'm not used to that.

Alejandro's experience illustrates the institutionalized meanings and intersected identity frames others, such as police officers, draw upon to label men of color as more dangerous. Within the criminal justice system, certain social positions are more stigmatized, and socially visible, than others. Individuals within the system rely on these institutional stereotypes to inform their interactions with those who occupy, or are attributed, that intersecting identity frame. Fourteen of the Latino, Black, and multiracial trans men interviewed reported experiencing greater stigmatization by police officers after transitioning, regardless of social class.

Within online forums and informal discussions at conferences, trans men of color reiterated this experience of increased surveillance by police. Steve (Black trans man) shared: "as a man of color, you're moving into a class of being a significant threat to other people. While you aren't necessarily a threat, that's going to be assigned to you." This assignment is, in part, due to broader institutionalized hegemonic stereotypes and the policies stemming from them. For instance, compared to white men, Black men are more likely to be under surveillance and punished for "bad" behavior (Morris 2005; Siegel 2020). Although these experiences

48 Transgender Intersections

of increased surveillance of men of color are not a revelation, Black, Indigenous, and other trans men of color shared their initial surprise when this new intersected identity frame was being attributed to them. They addressed how resources from (white) trans communities did not adequately prepare them for this.

The stigmatization of men of color as criminals by officers did not decrease even when trans men's status as transgender was disclosed. Their accounts reveal that officers tend to respond in two ways. In an informal grouping at a trans conference, one Black trans man, just beginning his transition, shared being pulled over by the police "for no specific reason." The officer's response, after reading his former name and gender marker ("F" for female) on his driver's license, was to "further harass" him.

A second response is exemplified in Steve's story. Steve, a middle-class Black trans man living in California, was pulled over by an officer for a traffic violation. When this occurred, Steve was relatively new in his transition and appeared much younger than his actual age; additionally, although initially perceived as a man by the officer, he had an "F" marker on his driver's license. Steve emphasized that when he was pulled over, he responded the same way he had when perceived as a Black woman, by driving to a place he felt "safe" to stop:

[I made] the same decisions I would make as a woman, and not recognizing how that decision being made and me being perceived as male looks to the police, and the realization is that no benefit of the doubt was being put in my direction whatsoever . . . I am a Black man who has been to jail, although I was on the women's side. (They put you on the women's side?) . . . My driver's license said female so they had to put me on the women's side. They couldn't put me on the men's side. (I talked to a couple of white trans men who deliberately leave an "F" because then they won't be put in jail, I mean depending

> on the situation. . .). Oh, no, there was no doubt that they were
> sending me to jail . . . This guy was so pissed off. Pulled over
> for speeding, I didn't pull over when he wanted me to . . . And
> the cop just absolutely lost his mind. I perceived it as a safety
> concern and he perceived it as "a belligerent Black man not
> doing what I tell you to do" situation.

Steve believed the officer's anger came from the latter's interpretation of his choice to keep driving as not being about personal safety, but rather as a sign of him being a "belligerent Black man." Steve did not believe his status as transgender affected the officer's response. This is significant because while there was documentation to support Steve's story (e.g., an "F" on his driver's license), the officer refused to take this into account, maintaining the initial intersecting identity frame until he was imprisoned on the women's side. Moreover, this contrasts with the narrative from some white trans men who shared strategically keeping the "F" on their driver's license in an attempt to prevent them from going to jail.

As was the case for Steve, Alejandro, and the conference participant, other Black, Indigenous, and trans men of color shared concerns and experiences suggesting that officers rely and act on intersecting identity frames of men of color as more dangerous. We can further interrogate these intersecting identity frames by using the intersectional model to analyze the plane of gender expression. One conference participant, a masculine of center Latina, whose driver's license (F) matched her gender identity, shared a similar story to Steve's. She was pulled over by the police, assumed to be and interacted with as a man of color, and then experienced further harassment when the officer discovered she was a woman who was gender nonconforming. Considering gender along a multifaceted plane rather than in terms of a binary understanding reveals more complex intersections and some of the ways these are rooted in settler white normativity.

50   Transgender Intersections

Even in cases where trans men interact in the criminal justice system as employees or observers, stigmatized social positions are often assigned. Jacobo continually dealt with subtle and explicit racialized, classed, gendered, and sexualized stereotypes of Latinos, as well as assumptions around language and nationality – directed both towards himself and Latinos as a group – by co-workers and clients. His presence as Latino *and* a legal investigator seemed problematic for others; both clients and court employees often mistook him for a client. To advance professionally in the criminal justice system, Jacobo had to consistently resist and challenge these stereotypes. Jacobo's experiences of others' interactions with him were heightened as a heterosexual Latino versus when he had been formerly perceived as a lesbian Latina. Jacobo believed that, prior to transition, when he was perceived as a lesbian Latina, he was often socially invisible to others, which was problematic in other ways; however, his visible presence as a Latino particularly within a legal setting (e.g., court room) is initially framed by others' stereotypes of Latinos as criminals, increasing his social visibility.

Jacobo revealed similar experiences in terms of the way others connected his social class with being perceived as Latino. Even though others utilize normative definitions of middle class for most people, Latinos are often assumed to be poor or working class (Vasquez-Tokos 2020). Jacobo deliberately wore suits and ties to his job and other places and events to counter this stereotype; he noted: "People are surprised to see that I'm a Latino male with a Bachelor's degree and not involved in a gang." Even in a suit, working in the criminal justice field, Jacobo was occasionally mistaken for a defendant, particularly by white people: "I was in court one day with my suit and stuff so a [white] guy said 'what are you here for?' . . . and I said, 'Actually I'm with the defense team. I'm probably representing you' (laughing)." This is consistent with white racial framing of Latinos as uneducated and laborers (Feagin and Corbes 2008), something all five Latino trans men shared that they experienced. To be taken seriously, Jacobo believed he needed to be more normative in his presentation. In his case, wearing suits allowed him to present a more middle-class, American identity associated with masculine white normativity, which situationally muted his stigmatized social position. This supports Morris's (2005) finding that, in school settings, educators were less likely to negatively stigmatize Latino boys who presented as middle class through particular clothing (e.g., Dockers pants). Trans men's accounts reveal the inequalities within the criminal justice system based on interconnecting social positions. These combined disparities, expressed as categorical hierarchies, become institutionalized and are realized by individuals within the system, thus further perpetuating perceptions of who is "good" and who is "bad."

Social invisibility and hypervisibility have significant consequences for trans people marked as non-white within a white supremacist society. It is important and sometimes vital to recognize how shifts in gender intersect with race through these processes of gendered racialization. Gendered racialization and social in/visibility highlight the ways an intersectional analysis connects people's lived experiences, identities, and social positions within systems of privilege and oppression that are rooted in societal institutions and social structures.

Intersectional Accounts of Trans People's Lives

These narratives from Black, Indigenous, and other trans people of color reveal some of the ways race, ethnicity, social class, gender, sexuality, body size, nationality, and language interconnect and are attributed institutionalized meanings by others; how these are hierarchical categorizations based on hegemonic narratives and normative expectations; and how they are experienced, performed, and resisted by trans people. When a person subscribes to these meanings, as with Jake's belief that his middle-class white normative behaviors improved relations with his co-workers, their structural opportunities potentially increase. Resistance can also be a powerful tool, as in the ways Katrice and Josie resisted exclusion from white normative trans spaces by creating resources for themselves and other Black trans people. Regardless of whether people embody these normative behaviors or not, the structural barriers are differentially permeable based on their interconnecting social positions.

Trans people's lived experiences offer rich analysis about our society. Trans people in the USA who transition do so in relation to androcentric, heteronormative, middle-class, white normative cultural narratives. These dominant narratives shape the meanings we attach to different social locational identities, which combine in various ways to frame interaction. Although all people must engage with the intersected identity frames others attach to them, many specific combinations are foregrounded in the context of transitioning.

Drawing from these interviews with Black, Indigenous, and other trans people of color, we find that the meanings others attach to interconnections of race, social class, gender, and sexuality vary in their combination and shape interactions. Furthermore, expanding on Lewis (2004) and Ward (2008), who make evident the importance of analyzing dominant cultural narratives such as whiteness, we highlight the interconnections of class and sexuality which influence a participant's perceived gender.

This marks an important move towards an intersectional analysis of identities in interaction. Identity literature in sociological social psychology suggests that certain "singular" social identities are more salient for individuals, depending on the interaction. We attend to the ways race, social class, gender, and sexuality combine and are used to attribute specific intersected identity frames in interaction. This provides an empirical example of intersected identity frames and demonstrates an analysis that reveals the complexity of these frames, the creativity of social actors, and the numerous ways these play out in social interaction.

Finally, we note three ways in which this research advances our understanding of identities in interaction. First, it demonstrates how people draw upon dominant and racial/ethnic cultural narratives about race, class, gender, and sexuality to identify, code, and frame their interactions with others. Second, it suggests ways people incorporate the intersected identity frame others attribute to them. For participants, this begins with learning about the new frame being attributed to them in a process of accountable conduct (Connell 2009). In some cases, this new frame is identity confirming; however, in many cases, participants were surprised by some of the meanings attributed to them. For instance, the change in intersected identity frame experienced during and/or after transitioning sometimes results in trans people gaining or losing social visibility. Once they learned these new frames, participants engaged in various management and negotiation techniques. Third, this research illustrates the powerful influence of attributed intersected identity frames on an individual's sense of self. For the participants, being legitimated in their gender entailed understanding themselves through these intersecting attributions.

The overarching meanings people attribute to each other in relation to race, class, gender, and sexuality in interaction matter greatly in our social world. These meanings are not only experienced by trans people; rather, trans people's experiences illuminate the complex intersections of race, class, gender, and sexuality. While some audiences employ white normative narratives, others draw upon other racial and ethnic cultural narratives. In all cases, transitioning throws the multidimensionality of intersected identity frames into sharp relief against the background of intersecting social and cultural structural arrangements.

3

Multiraciality

Diego asked to have his interview at his home on the west coast. We sit in his apartment sipping coffee and make some small talk. He signals he is ready for the interview to begin, and I ask him to start by sharing a little about himself. With some nervous laughter, he shares that he is almost twenty-five and started transitioning when he was nineteen. The reason Diego volunteered to be part of the study, and what he was excited to share with me, was how others perceived him as a white girl and later as a white woman growing up, but as he transitioned in relation to his gender and people began to acknowledge him as a man, shifts occurred in how others perceived his race as well. Diego explained that he is "half-Irish and half-Puerto Rican," but grew up in the foster care system which had him documented only as "white." In fact, until transitioning, Diego thought of himself as just white:

This chapter is derived in part from the article "Transitioning Gender, Transitioning Race: Transgender People and Multiracial Positionality" by Kylan Mattias de Vries and Carey Jean Sojka, published in *International Journal of Transgender Health* in 2022 © Taylor and Francis Group, available online: http://www.tandfonline.com/10.1080/26895269.2020.1838388. Reprinted by permission of Taylor and Francis Group.

It wasn't really a part of a racial identity as much as this kind of mix of two cultures, kind of coming together that I kind of never thought about growing up. I don't think I really became conscious of my race until . . . eighteen . . . and as I transitioned, just how things shifted for me.

It was through daily interactions with others reflecting back to him that they no longer perceived him as white that Diego underwent a shift in how he experienced his ethnic and racial identity, which was also intimately connected to assumptions about his nationality. For Diego, this was a shift to being attributed a "Brown" identity; it prompted his acknowledgement of his Puerto Rican ethnicity, but in a racialized way. Exploring how gender shifts impact racial shifts such as the one Diego experienced helps us to understand the intimate interactions between race and gender for trans people.

If race is gendered and gender is racialized, what does that mean for trans people who live, or are perceived as living, between racial categories, or for trans people who inhabit multiple racial and/or ethnic categories at once? The experiences of multiracial trans people demonstrate particular interconnections between race and gender and the ways these categories influence each other when one is perceived to be in flux. In this chapter, we focus on the stories of multiracial and multiethnic transgender people who shared shifting experiences of race as they transitioned gender. The embodied markers others drew upon to ascribe a racial identity to these participants are interconnected with gender, sexuality, and nationality, which are rooted in relationships of power. These intersectional identity attributions had a profound effect on participants' sense of self, their perceptions of fluidity and "borderlands" (Anzaldúa 2007), and their experiences of inequity.

Multiracial Positionality

While research about multiracial (i.e., mixed-race, biracial, mixed-heritage, or interracial) individuals spans centuries (Ifekwunigwe 2004), critical mixed-race studies (CMRS) has more recently been recognized as its own interdisciplinary field (Daniel et al. 2014). Much of this work has been informed by Omi and Winant's "racial formation theory" (1994:109) and the process of racialization, or the ways in which racial meaning is attributed to individuals, groups, social practices, and/or relationships. In the USA, and arguably elsewhere, this process is integral to the structure and organization of society and individual lives. While race is not a biologically deterministic category, bodies and physical characteristics (e.g., phenotype, skin color, hair style and color) are socially imbued with racial meaning (Omi and Winant 1994). Scholarship has often focused on how the existence of multiracial individuals calls into question the hegemony of monolithic understandings of race or "the depiction of racialization as monolithic" (Curington 2016:27). Some CMRS addresses how identities are intersectional and complex and how individuals incorporate and resist societal definitions of race and ethnicity (Cerezo et al. 2020; Curington 2016; Garrett 2024; Khanna 2004; for an in-depth review of CMRS, see Daniel et al. 2014).

In defining CMRS, Daniel et al. describe a critical process where multiracial people

> become subjects of historical, social, and cultural processes rather than simply objects of analysis. This involves the study of racial consciousness among racially mixed people, the world in which they live, and the ideological, social, economic, and political forces, as well as policies that impact the social location of mixed-race individuals and inform their mixed-race experiences and identities. CMRS also stresses the critical analysis of the institutionalization of social, cultural, and political

structures based on dominant conceptions of "race." . . . CMRS also emphasizes the interlocking nature of racial phenomena with gender, sex, sexuality, class, and other categories of difference. (2014:8)

This intersectional approach highlights the importance of broader power structures in creating and reinforcing the meaning attributed to identities and social locations. Khanna used Cooley's ([1902] 1964) framework of "reflected appraisals" to highlight the ways multiracial individuals reflected on what racial identity was attributed to them in interaction, in turn shaping their own sense of self and racial identity (2004:116). Khanna found phenotype or physical appearance and cultural exposure significantly influenced how individuals began to think about their racial self. While Khanna did not find that gender influenced an individual's racial identity, individuals in the study may not have been aware of how gender interacted as an intersecting identity frame. Additionally, while few studies address changes in embodied racial markers for multiracial individuals over time, Khanna noted:

Some respondents commented on how their racial identity was influenced by changes in their looks while they were growing up. Their comments directly link their perception of others towards their looks to their own racial identity. More important, these comments connect others' reactions to their looks to how others *interacted* with them, which in turn affected how the respondents identified. (2004:125, emphasis in original)

These "reflected appraisals" can significantly factor into the interactions and experiences of multiracial people, influencing not just how others perceive them, but also how they perceive themselves.

In part because the people in the present study engaged in various medical transition processes, how they were perceived

58   Transgender Intersections

by others shifted over time. We suggest the importance of examining this shift from an intersectional lens, with particular attention to broader ideologies, narratives, and power structures, as we investigate the relationship between gender and race. These experiences with others had a profound effect on participants' sense of self and identity.

Transitioning Shifts

Transition can correlate with and lead to a change in gender attribution and how we learn to do, enact, and embody gender (Dozier 2005). While not all trans people experience transition or aspects of transition in the same way, many participants in our study predominantly experienced a shift from being perceived by others as one gender to another, regardless of their gender identities over time, and, to varying degrees, some conceived of gender as fluid. For them, the concept of transitioning gender typically meant altering mannerisms and appearance coded as gendered, taking hormones resulting in bodily changes, and in some cases having one or more gender-affirming surgeries.

While participants expected their perceived gender to change throughout transition, they did not anticipate that this might also mean a shift in how others, and often they themselves, perceived their race.[2] Because the social construction of race is rooted in embodied meanings which are strongly linked to other social positions such as gender (Collins 2000;

---

[2] This differs from so-called "transracial" claims. The experiences in this chapter are from people who are multiracial or multiethnic and are responding to shifting monoracial perceptions from others of their non-monoracial experience, particularly when these changing perceptions are linked to their gender transitions. Their experiences demonstrate that race is not fixed and is a social construction, but their experiences do not demonstrate that racial identities can be arbitrarily chosen.

Combahee River Collective 1995; Crenshaw 1991), it makes sense that trans people who experience changes in their gender embodiment and in how others perceive their gender may experience shifts in other intersecting categories. Participants experienced both rigid and fluid shifts in how their race was perceived by others throughout their gender transition. Rigid shifts are not concrete but instead indicate more consistent attributions (e.g., predominantly changing from attributions of one racial category to another). In contrast, fluid shifts indicate how racialized gender attributions can change not only across transition but also across multiple contexts before, during, and after transition.

Rigid Shifts

The multiracial/multiethnic trans people's experiences in this study demonstrate how socially constructed racialized gender meanings are intersectional. Three participants, Diego, Scout, and Lance, experienced more rigid shifts in others' racial perceptions of them as they transitioned gender:

Diego: white woman → Latino/Brown man
Scout: white woman → Latino/Brown man
Lance: woman/man of color → white man (Indigenous man in Indigenous communities)

As each of these participants transitioned gender, their shifts in body/facial hair and hair style/length, in combination with height, hair color, skin color, and other embodied markers, were used by others to ascribe a new racialized gender.

Diego, a twenty-four-year-old queer trans man living on the west coast, stated that prior to transition he "passed for white" (i.e., he was treated as white); "people didn't pick up on the fact that I'm Puerto Rican . . . I actually grew up in the foster system, and I looked up my court papers recently and they listed me as [non-Hispanic] white." He did not become "conscious of my race until eighteen" because he had been predominantly perceived as white, which is common in that many white people do not think of themselves as having a race, reserving racial identity for non-white people (Bonilla-Silva 2003).

However, when discussing his gender transition, Diego stated: "I think the most interesting thing that changed for me [after transition] is my ethnicity is much more easily read." Some scholars are increasingly analyzing a Brown racialized experience, sometimes in relation to Latinx identity and sometimes in relation to other racial identities (Galarte 2021; Heidenreich 2020; Luibheid and Chávez 2020; Rizki 2019). While Diego is discussing his ethnicity being perceived by others, this is additionally happening through a process of racialization or "being Brown" in intersection with trans experience. Diego identified ways that others signaled they now perceived him as non-white:

> I work at farmer's markets, and I work for a farm, and people automatically, even if I go to a grocery store, automatically will speak to me in Spanish. And they're people who are not native Spanish speakers. And that never happened before. Ever.

In noting that this "never happened before" his transition, Diego highlights the intersecting perceptions from others that shifted during his gender transition. The people who began to interact with him in these ways were "not native Spanish speakers" and were predominantly white and non-Latinx; Sims also found that when a multiethnic individual was perceived to be Latinx, "the main indicator was that Spanish was automatically spoken to them" (2016:577). Through language, white people attributed "otherness" (e.g., Latinx ≠ American), demonstrating that perceived citizenship hinges on embodying whiteness (Haritaworn 2009).

Multiraciality   61

Diego's experience highlights some of the complexities of the Latinx ethnic category and its overlap with a racialized experience:

> Latinx refers foremost to an ethnic identity that is often associated with a Brown racial identity, but it can also refer to a white or Black racial identity, as well as an indigenous identity (not to mention how multiraciality complicates this simple schema). Latinx is an inherently inter-locking category, overtly signaling attentiveness to coloniality, ethnicity and gender, and implicitly pointing to race and sexuality. (Soto Vega and Chávez 2018:320)

Vasquez addresses the social experience within the Latinx category, suggesting a continuum from "flexible ethnicity" – the ability to "navigate different racial terrains and be considered an 'insider' in more than one racial or ethnic group" – to the racialization as non-white (2010:46). Some of the concerns in equating ethnicity and race are that it conflates distinctions within this racially heterogeneous group, potentially minimizes colorism, and may not address the vulnerability of "Latinxs who are visibly othered (e.g., skin color, phenotype)" (Chavez-Dueñas, et al. 2019:51). However, this is further complicated by white nationalist ideology and rhetoric which simultaneously frame Latinx as non-white and un-American, regardless of one's racial identification. When Diego and some of the other participants talk about their ethnicity being "more easily read" or being perceived as Latinx, they are referring to others racializing them as non-white. These participants interpreted this as a shared Brown racial experience and identity.

Diego was fairly consistently perceived as Brown after transition, but he noted one instance in which he was temporarily perceived as white. In an African American Studies class, he was one of only three non-Black people in the classroom. He challenged a comment another student made about people speaking "Mexican," pointing out that Spanish as a language and Mexican as a nationality are not interchangeable. Later, classmates asked him his ethnicity, and when he said he was Puerto Rican, they responded "Oh! We thought you were white!" In the context of both Latinx and white communities, Diego was perceived as Brown, but here the Black–white divide may have factored into racial attributions more. This situation, and Diego's early discussion of his ethnicity being perceived as non-white, aligns with Gonzales's finding that in "everyday life, being Latina [or in this case Latino] and white are seen as mutually exclusive, especially when one has lighter skin color and can pass as white" (2019:7). In other words, once marked as Latino by his classmates, they interacted with Diego as non-white.

Like Diego, Scout also experienced a shift from being perceived as white to Brown. Scout is a twenty-three-year-old "genderqueer, butch, trannyboi, dyke-fag, puppy-boy, daddy" living on the west coast who was adopted and raised by conservative, white Jewish parents. Although he is Cuban/white and would "get pretty dark, especially in the summer," as he grew up, he had thought of himself as white, was perceived by others as white, and his parents spoke minimally about racial/ethnic identity while growing up. Scout mentioned he was shorter, which he felt was not typically perceived as masculine, but he also became "very hairy" early in his gender transition. Because of stereotypes of Latino men as short, his height in combination with his dark and thick facial and body hair combined to increase others' acceptance of him as a (Brown) man. He commented: "the more and more I pass [as a man], the more I felt like I was read as a Hispanic male," and as a result, he's "identifying with it more and more." In this sense, Scout wasn't being perceived as racially white and ethnically Latinx, but what Soto Vega and Chávez (2018) refer to as being racialized as Brown. With this attribution came negative interactions from white people; Scout noted that, after transition, "people treat me as if I'm part of that [Latino] stereotype."

Multiraciality 63

Scout and Diego both discussed moving from a normative white racial experience to being perceived as a racial threat. Scout shared his first experience of this shift:

> I never thought about being an interracial couple before. When I was with [white girlfriend] I would get looks ... like, "Why are you dating a white girl?" when it wasn't a problem [before transitioning] because everyone just read me as white.

Scout's experience aligns with many men of color in the USA who are hypersexualized and perceived as threats to white women (Nagel 2003). Scout's and Diego's experiences also align with what Rivera refers to as a "Brown threat" (2014:45), where Brown bodies, despite racial and cultural heterogeneity, are imagined as a national threat, and those labeled as Brown typically share an experience of "racialization and securitization" by the white American imaginary (2014:49). Rivera argues that the "[Brown threat] ... highlights an ideological construction in the United States that suggests a difference from and a danger to the current definition of white(ness) as indicative of European descent or of Black(ness) as indicative of African descent" (2014:46). Similar to the racial othering of Scout and Diego by white people in terms of language, this framing of a Brown threat further emphasizes the broader sociopolitical meanings of American as white.

These newer experiences of being racialized as Brown had a significant effect on how Diego and Scout thought about their own racial identities. Scout noted: "not only am I transitioning into my gender, I'm claiming my ethnic background," and he also started identifying as Brown. As these participants transitioned, it was only through reflected appraisals (Khanna 2004) that they began to understand aspects of their racial identities in new ways. Their internalization and incorporation of others' perceptions of their racialized identity involved more than claiming a particular label/category; they began to construct and "do" race in ways that aligned with how people treated them, including changing their racial identification. Based on these continued interactions, Diego and Scout incorporated aspects of others' shifting perceptions of their racial and ethnic identities, for example by becoming involved in Latinx communities, beginning to learn Spanish, and identifying as Brown.

These shifts, while empowering for Diego and Scout in some ways, also brought other challenges. While Scout was learning how to navigate the world being perceived as a man of color, he said he often still felt "like an outsider" in people of color spaces because his multiracial identity had previously been perceived by others as white. He was also now sometimes treated as an outsider in predominantly white queer communities because he was perceived as a Brown man. Scout talked about attending a queer play party – a BDSM sex party, that may or may not involve sex – for cis women and trans people where two white trans men confronted him, saying "you're a [cis]man. You're not supposed to be here." Scout's racialized gender was assumed to be cis; as a Brown man, Scout's shorter height and his amount of dark body hair were interpreted as cis by white normative trans standards. Scout added, "I feel like it's a lot easier for me to pass as a bio male because I'm Brown . . . Because I'm short and white men are tall." Scout's experience further exemplifies how others draw on intersected identity frames, informed by hegemonic ideologies and narratives, to mark bodies and frame interactions.

In contrast to Diego and Scout, Lance's transition shifted other's perceptions of his race towards whiteness. Lance, a mixed-heritage (Assiniboine (Nakoda), Cherokee, and white) trans and intersex man living in the Midwest, said he grew up "in the middle," being somewhat socialized as a girl by one parent and as a boy by the other. Particularly after puberty, his embodiment, both through his gender socialization from his parents and from other aspects such as hormones (e.g., having a goatee prior to taking testosterone), positioned him

Multiraciality 65

in the borderlands of gender, being sometimes perceived as a woman and other times as a man (Anzaldúa 2007). As "mixed-heritage," Lance stated he aligned with a quote from Cherríe Moraga: "I am a woman with a foot in both worlds; and I refuse the split" (2015:29). For Lance, his refusal of the split referred to his race, his gender, and his Indigeneity.

Lance's experiences of being intersex, transgender, and mixed-heritage all influenced how he understood the world; he commented: "To me, there's always this duality. It's even more than a duality; it's sort of like this multiplicity of who people are and that's not confusing to me. It's like, of course that's how everybody works." Lance also recognized racialized gender processes as socially constructed:

> I actually have the privilege to see both sides, so I see that both sides of gender are constructions. Just like race is a construction . . . 'cause if you can look at me and tell me I'm completely white, well, that's interesting, because you constructed for yourself what white looks like.

As with all the participants, others racialized Lance through a process of assigning phenotypic characteristics to mark bodies along lines of race/ethnicity. This process of "knowing" which phenotypic characteristics to apply to which race/ethnicity is informed by intersectional hegemonic meanings, particularly around ideas of whiteness (Chavez-Dueñas et al. 2019). Lance experienced this in two ways. Living in a predominantly white rural area, he grew up being treated as a racial other. As discussed in Chapter 1, he stated:

> When I was a kid I'd always have people ask me, "What are you?" They'd look at me and think I was Asian, which is pretty common. People often think that Native Americans are Asian, because of our eyes and stuff like that . . . And it's been interesting in the transition, 'cause my facial structure has changed so

> much that I don't get that question as often as I used to. 'Cause
> my cheek bones don't look the same, my face has gotten whiter.

Lance was not referring to the color of his skin becoming lighter; rather, people were drawing on other visual cues that now marked him as racially white.

Lance knew this shift in racial marking was happening because of changes in how people interacted with him. He discussed how, after transition, in his work environment among predominantly Black and Hmong folks, he was consistently perceived as non-Native and white, although he would still be perceived as Native in Indigenous communities. As he socially shifted to being perceived more predominantly as a white man, a more dominant social position, he continued to work in, but mostly removed himself socially from, areas where people of color were more prevalent. A key change for him was that both white people and non-Indigenous people of color no longer perceived him as a person of color after his transition; thus, his experiences of racism as a child, for example, were rendered not "real" by others. Unlike Diego and Scout, who somewhat embraced being racialized as Brown, Lance resisted being racialized as white and struggled with how to challenge his perceived and attributed masculine white privilege. In addition, his now being marked as predominantly white by others discounted Lance's Native identity and brought up historical and contemporary trauma of Indigenous people being erased through settler colonialism.

These three participants experienced a racialized gender shift in how others perceived them that was fairly consistent. As a result, they also incorporated others' perceptions into their sense of self, which emphasizes the importance of meanings attached to embodiment of racialized gender.

Multiraciality

Fluid Shifts

While Diego's, Scout's, and Lance's experiences of race shifted through their gender transition, the shifts were more rigid than not. However, three other multiracial/multiethnic participants found that perceptions of their race also shifted but continued to remain in flux depending on their location, setting, and who was perceiving them.

Bennyboy: Filipina/o ↔ Latina/o
Dexter: white woman/man ↔ Latina/o
Morgan: Native American man ↔ white woman

Bennyboy is a twenty-eight-year-old baklâ, queer "Puertopino" (Puerto Rican/Filipino), born in the Philippines and now living in the southwest USA. He commented that his baklâ identity provides a cultural connection to his Filipino roots and aligns with his feeling of being both genders. According to Manalansan, "Bakla is a [pejorative and sometimes reclaimed] Tagalog sexual/gender category still prevalent in contemporary Philippines today" (2015:113). Bennyboy had lived in the southwest and west USA, the Philippines, and Japan, and his location influenced racial attributions from others. Even within the USA, regional location shapes racial classifications and social experiences (Soto Vega and Chávez 2018). Bennyboy shared that in the southwest, people "thought I was Mexican, just because we're really close to Mexico," and people did not think he was Asian "because there's not really many Asian people here." However, when he lived on the west coast, "people are like, 'you look Puerto Rican and Filipino' and they're dead on," which he attributed to the larger Filipino population in that location.

Bennyboy's shifting embodiment, related to the effects of taking testosterone, was intimately connected to his regional racialized experiences and profoundly affected his sense of self.

68   Transgender Intersections

His struggle to integrate others' racial attributions with his self-understandings is what Vargas and Kingsbury refer to as "racial identity contestation" (2016:719). In thinking about how others now perceived him racially, he reflected on his gender transition, noting "it's really important for me to realize it was a choice that I made to physically change my being, outside at least." Although he was coming to terms with the fluidity of how others racialized him, his identity as Puertopino, and not racial fluidity, was a significant part of his sense of self.

Dexter, like Bennyboy, also lived in the southwest. Dexter is a twenty-seven-year-old FTM who grew up primarily with his white mother but spent time with his "dark-skinned" Mexican American father and grandmother. Dexter shared: "as I've gotten older, my skin's whitened a lot, but when I was younger, my skin was darker." This may, in part, be due to his spending less time as an adult in the sun, in contrast to Lance's experience of having others utilize additional phenotypic markers to attribute whiteness. Dexter said his father's family highly valued assimilation into white culture, and his father raised him to believe he should "be as white as you can." Dexter's father's advice is based on both assimilationism and experiences of colorism: the "social inequities circumscribed by skin color gradients within racial and ethnic groups" that support the broader racialized system in the USA (Burton et al. 2010:440).

Dexter utilized testosterone for about a year, which altered his features and voice; he noted that he is most often perceived as masculine (the exception was when he was with his taller, queer, white girlfriend). Although Dexter experienced his childhood racialized as Brown, as an adult his experience was more fluid; he stated: "a lot of white people perceive me as white, and Latino people perceive me as Latino." While now lighter skinned and perceived more often as white, Dexter's assumptions of ingroup recognition as Latinx were tied to his thinking of "us Brown folk." This experience of racial fluidity

Multiraciality   69

from childhood to adulthood, and of changes in attribution by others depending on the audience, significantly shaped how he understood his gender. He shared that his "transness" was "almost comfortable at this point, like someone that's in the borderland of race and gender . . . I've always been between races; I've never belonged to either." Dexter's understanding about the fluidity of his race and gender, as well as Lance's experiences, are similar to what Anzaldúa refers to as "mestiza consciousness" (2007:112): occupying the borderland, holding a dual consciousness, and embracing ambiguity and contradictions. Dexter's multiracial/multiethnic experience thus helped him to be more comfortable with his gender transition.

Dexter appreciated both his racial and gender fluidity and had stopped taking testosterone so as to curtail its more "masculinizing" effects. His embodied gender changes through transition influenced how others perceived and related to his racialized gender. Dexter noted: "The first lover I had after transitioning, she very much saw me as Latino, and she was, like, really into that, really exoticizing the Latinoness. And that was a whole new experience for me, being the Latin lover" (see Lie 2014). Dexter's shifting experiences of racialized gender through transition thus influenced how others perceived him in intimate and sexual relationships.

Like Bennyboy and Dexter, Morgan also experienced fluid shifts. Morgan is a twenty-three-year-old who is "genderqueer, [a] trans-dyke, multiracial," living on the west coast, and the child of white lesbian parents. The sperm donor her mothers chose is Native/Chicano and someone Morgan met in adulthood. Although growing up she knew she was multiracial, "half-Chicana," and Indigenous, it wasn't until she was sixteen that she really considered her racial identity. Morgan said she has "an ability to pass as white, and so even when people aren't assuming that I'm white, they are thinking 'maybe she could be.'"

Morgan noted that for a long time, she felt she had to

> trade off as either being seen as a person of color or being seen
> as trans or female . . . What that meant is I had very long hair,
> and when people saw me as being Native, then that was the
> reason why I had long hair, and then of course they saw me
> and my gender in a way that I didn't want to be seen. And so if
> I went into white spaces and passed as white, then I could pass
> as a woman a lot better. It actually really unfortunately drove
> me away from the Native community.

In response, she said, "I ended up cutting my hair and started passing as female a lot better [with] short hair, and I think part of it was being read as Native . . . It seems like the higher my hair goes, the more I pass." Morgan's experience, that either her gender or her race/Indigeneity would be validated but not both, demonstrates how multiracial/multiethnic trans experience can come with unique challenges. It further emphasizes the importance of examining embodiment through the construction of racial and gender identities and social positions (Gonzales 2019).

While multiracial people are often not affirmed in asserting a multiracial identity and are pushed into monoracial categories, some can move across racial categories (Gonzales 2019). For the people in this study, experiences of moving across categories of race and gender influenced each other. As Morgan stated: "beginning to realize that one person would see me as a person of color and another person see me as white in the same moment gave me the ability to start thinking about my gender in similar terms." Thus, some multiracial trans people can draw connections between the fluidity of race and the fluidity of gender that influence their understandings of both social categories and how they understand their identities.

Implications of Shifting Race

These shifting experiences of race reveal the continued significance of marking the racial other to maintain current racial, gendered, and national boundaries. Furthermore, this suggests that intersections of gender with race, sexuality, and nationality are key to this marking (Nagel 2003). This confirms that challenging normative subject positions in the USA, and arguably elsewhere, requires an intersectional approach, and that in trans studies particularly, we must attend to the ways the concept of transition implicates not only gender, but also other categories such as race and nationality.

Others' perceptions shape our experiences of our identities and the social understanding of race as well as gender. Multiracial/multiethnic transgender people's experiences provide valuable insight into the construction and fluidity of racial identities. Participants' experiences demonstrate first and most significantly the importance of intersectional analysis and that the social construction of race is rooted in embodied meanings strongly linked to other social positions such as gender, sexuality, and nationality. Second, participants' integration of the ways others perceive their racial identities reveals the fluidity of these categories. Third, participants' experiences of gender as fluid or shifting shaped their understanding of race as fluid or shifting and vice versa. Finally, experiences of inequity significantly changed upon shifting experiences of both gender and race, which demonstrates how racialized gender identity meanings are rooted in relations of power. Because these shifts happened to participants in adulthood, they were able to recognize and interrogate the changes in social meanings attributed to them by others in interaction. Experiences of both rigid and fluid shifts provide a particular epistemic advantage to understanding both gender and race as intersecting social constructions rooted in systems of power.

The white normativity of transgender narratives erases the significant ways other social positions such as race intersect with gender to shape interactions and identities. For these multiracial/multiethnic trans participants, unexpected changes in their experiences of racialized gender often surprised them, and they initially felt unprepared because no one they knew had discussed this within trans communities. While we do not suggest this is the experience of all multiracial trans people, a focus on these experiences can challenge both white and monoracial normativity within transgender narratives and transform key understandings in transgender studies.

4

Whiteness

April invited me to her home on the west coast for her interview. It was a warm day, and we sat together in her living room sipping sparkling water. She had completed a demographic survey beforehand, and I opened the conversation with some questions expanding on what she had written. About half an hour into the interview, we got to the section on race and ethnicity, where she had written "Caucasian" as her racial identity. The demographic survey included racial categories; "white" was listed, not "Caucasian," but there was an "other" category where participants could write in their own terms. Caucasian is a contested term; the word is "a remnant of a discredited theory of racial classification" that perpetuates the "false idea that races are naturally occurring" (Mukhopadhyay 2008:12). "Using the word Caucasian," Mukhopadhyay argues, "also tends to imply that whites (the two terms are often used interchangeably) differ from other major racial groupings in the United States in being just plain Americans whose immigrant origins remain unmarked" (2008:14).

I used April's racial term of choice, as I did for everyone, to ask her what it was like to be Caucasian and trans in the

74 Transgender Intersections

area she lived in. She stated that the "area is predominantly Caucasian," and then took a long pause before beginning to share her discomfort with a local trans leadership group she was involved in:

> I find in the group that I mentioned, that I am involved in, part of the reason that I feel isolated from that group is that there's this really strong identity politics, kind of [a] normative structure to it, in terms of really heavily identifying with race, and really heavily identifying with grievance about race.

This trans group was composed predominantly of white trans people who were attempting to address the implications of their own whiteness, their experiences of white privilege, and how they might dismantle the system of white supremacy in their own lives and communities. April framed the focus on antiracism as "grievance about race" and felt that addressing race wasn't significantly relevant to their work on trans issues. She spoke for some time about her frustrations in feeling pushed to address her own white privilege through the group, referring to the group's attempted intersectional trans politics as an "oppression Olympics." She stated:

> I guess for me, that's also why I put down Caucasian. I don't wanna identify as white. I think it's a toxic term. I think the history of whiteness has to do with white supremacy, and white power, and I also feel this pressure, like it's not okay with other people if I don't wanna identify as white. There's almost this message of "you have to identify as white" 'cause of all these reasons, and this is kinda like your punishment, is to recognize that you have all this privilege.

April felt that her experience as a white trans person is removed from structures of white supremacy and that white privilege did not apply to her experience. She continued:

Whiteness 75

I really think the amount of white privilege is really overstated, like the assumption that I have all this power is . . . I don't experience having a lot of power. I understand such things as, like, just the difference between being able to move through the world, and not have the level of fear of police, suppose if I were a Black person. That's a huge difference, and that's something that's called a privilege. I guess in my mind, that's just a right that's being denied to Black people. It's not a privilege.

April recognized that racial oppression exists in our society, although she did not see herself as contributing to or maintaining that system. Instead, other people (such as the police, in the above quote) are the perpetrators of that oppression. By framing this issue around "rights" that everyone should have, she somewhat distanced herself from the concept of white privilege and from her own whiteness:

I think of a privilege as something that goes beyond your rights. And that's another problem I have with this whole language of privilege, is that I think a lot of things that are defined as white privilege are actually just rights that all people should have and should expect to have in a just society, rather than a privilege that comes at the expense of someone else. When I think of somebody who's rich, there's a privilege in wealth, because it comes at the expense of others who don't have that money . . . I want a different kind of life. I don't wanna make it according to our current society. I think our current society is irredeemable, like I don't think it works. I think it's destroying the planet. I think it's destroying our humanity. I think it's just tearing us into shreds, and so I never wanted to make it in that system. I didn't wanna be a placeholder of power in that system, so yeah, you asked about race, so I'm getting there in a roundabout way.

April was clear she did not want to be part of our current unjust and "toxic" system, but she articulated a largely "colorblind" approach to her own racial identity (Bonilla-Silva 2003). In taking this colorblind approach, she rhetorically distanced herself from holding any structural "power" or inhabiting racial privilege. Throughout the interview, she often returned to ideas of privilege and power and how she felt "alienated" in trans communities when other white trans people were having explicit conversations about racism, whiteness, and white supremacy. During the course of this research, she, and some other white trans participants, shared that they interpreted the naming of whiteness and white privilege as "racial victimhood" (Torkelson and Hartmann 2020).

It was clear that during our confidential interview April was sharing ideas about race that she did not share with the trans group or more publicly. I also believe that April assumed a certain racial camaraderie with me as a white researcher that led to her being comfortable sharing these ideas in a way that she would not have with an interviewer who was not white. While her story demonstrates that some (other) white trans people are engaged in discussions about whiteness in attempts to challenge white supremacy, it also shows how some white trans people like April resist recognizing their own white racial identities and habitus as part of systems of power. The intersectional prism suggests that social categories matter not just when they are experienced as marginalized in our society, but when they are structurally dominant or privileged as well, such as with whiteness. Recognizing and analyzing whiteness is a critical component in understanding the intersections between gender and race in the lives of trans people.

Critical Whiteness Studies and Trans Studies

Intersectionality stems from the work of Black women scholars, as we discussed in Chapter 1. While the framework comes out of analyses of marginalized experience, it is, of course, about challenging systems of power. Because of that, we know that those systems of power, and thus intersectionality, greatly matter when addressing dominant categories as well as marginalized ones. White supremacy and settler colonialism shape all trans people's lives in the USA, and in many other places, as systems of power. While not all white and/or settler trans people acknowledge it, they benefit from systems of white supremacy and colonization. Abelson's (2016a:1542) research on rural trans masculinity noted "the centrality of whiteness in making the claims to sameness that can make life better for a rural trans man and offer a clear economic advantage, even if they are individually opposed to this racism." Abelson demonstrates how whiteness and social class greatly shape trans men's experiences of gender and other social categories. We argue this is the case for white trans people across different geographies. The prism of intersectionality helps us to identify specific ways that whiteness and settler colonialism function in relation to trans experience.

It is a fairly common experience for white people, trans or cis, not to acknowledge how race shapes their own lives. Ahmed writes: "white bodies do not have to face their whiteness; they are not orientated 'towards' it, and this 'not' is what allows whiteness to cohere, as that which bodies are orientated around" (2007:156). In other words,

> whiteness remains so entirely hyper-visible as everything that it also becomes, paradoxically, invisible as nothing, the norm, as an invisible backdrop against which all other races are produced. It also means that whiteness was not a found category but one that was historically invented and/or constructed. (Noble 2006:89)

Moreover, in writing about his own transition, Noble notes: "The reading of a body as gendered male and racialized White involves presenting signifiers within an economy where the signifiers accumulate toward the appearance of a coherently gendered and racialized body" (2006:87). Some participants' whiteness was embodied through changes in gender identity and expression, along with shifts in community interactions, that resulted in some white trans people recognizing in a new way that they, too, held a racial identity. This leads us to question the ways in which trans experience can potentially help to orient some white people to their own whiteness, as well as why and how other trans people resist their own orientation towards whiteness.

This is not only the case for trans people, as Torkelson and Hartmann (2020:1) note: "More white Americans appear less oblivious to their status as white compared with prior times, and orientations toward white 'identity' now cover an ever-widening array of responses, emotions, and political implications." Like April, some participants resisted a recognition of their white identity, while others struggled with how to racially identify and/or grappled with their position in relation to inequity. Even for those who attempted to be accountable to their whiteness, their conversations often framed racism as a problem outside their social control; they didn't make personal changes to their racialized actions, nor did they participate in collective action to support BIPOC. There was very limited engagement among participants with how white trans people might be perpetuating exclusionary "white habitus" (Bonilla-Silva 2003).

In general, in the USA in the last couple of decades, white people have become somewhat more aware "not necessarily just about the privileges of whiteness or its embedded ideologies, but directly with respect to white identity and culture specifically" (Torkelson and Hartmann 2020:4). Coming into their gender identity resulted in some white trans and/or nonbinary folks contemplating their own whiteness and how whiteness factored into their experiences in new ways, while for others it made no difference. While some white participants had a sense of holding a white identity prior to identifying as trans

Whiteness 79

and/or transitioning, for many there was an awakening about having a racial identity and what that meant that occurred with some type of social or medically assisted transition. One way to understand why this shift might occur is to understand how white people create and maintain a white habitus – the "racialized, uninterrupted socialization process that conditions and creates white people's racial tastes, perceptions, feelings, and emotions and their views on racial matters" (Bonilla-Silva 2003:104; see also Ahmed 2007).

This white habitus is maintained through particular practices and interactions such as "speech patterns, gestures, principles of action, thought schemas" (Torkelson and Hartmann 2020:8). Lipsitz outlines what he refers to as the possessive investment in whiteness. He claims:

> Whiteness has a cash value: it accounts for advantages that come to individuals through profits made from housing secured in discriminatory markets, through the unequal educational opportunities available to children of different races, through insider networks that channel employment opportunities to the relatives and friends of those who have profited most from present and past discrimination, and especially through intergenerational transfers of inherited wealth that pass on the spoils of discrimination to succeeding generations. (2006:vii)

White people then benefit from adhering to the norms that continue to provide "them with resources, power, and opportunity" (Lipsitz 2006:vii). Matias and Boucher also find that "many folks *do* know a lot about how race and whiteness operate, yet strategically use this knowledge to feign innocence when committing racist acts in the hopes of escaping culpability" (2023:69, emphasis in original).

Whiteness is just as important a racial category to consider in analysis as other racial categories. In this chapter, we explore the meanings of whiteness to trans lives and experiences. We

80   Transgender Intersections

begin by centering the reflections of Black, Indigenous, and other trans people of color on whiteness and white habitus, and then we will also address white participants' experiences, reflections, and understandings.

Experiences with Whiteness

The ways whiteness shapes experience often go unmarked or unnoticed by white people precisely because whiteness is the dominant racial category, but whiteness is often quite apparent to people who do not hold white identities. Ahmed notes that "Whiteness could be described as an ongoing and unfinished history, which orientates bodies in specific directions, affecting how they 'take up' space" (2007:150). While many white trans people fail to recognize the ways in which their whiteness shapes their trans experience, and simultaneously how their trans experience shapes their experience of whiteness, trans BIPOC often have significant insight into the implications of whiteness.

BIPOC Analysis of Whiteness

Some trans BIPOC shared their experiences in relation to white habitus, for instance of growing up in predominantly white neighborhoods, communities, and education systems. Steve, a Black bisexual trans man, reflected on his experiences of growing up and continuing to reside in predominantly white spaces:

> So I am used to being in all white spaces almost, as it's how I grew up. So I talk about being the most visible invisible person in the room as "We will pretend like we don't see you, but we know where you are all the time." So you're constantly under surveillance. And I think that's just being Black in America,

Whiteness 81

as you are constantly under surveillance, especially when you show up places where [white] people don't expect to see you.

The shift to Black masculinity increased Steve's experiences of being "the most visible, invisible person." Since "spaces are orientated 'around' whiteness" (Ahmed 2007:157), BIPOC experience in white spaces can be hypervisible and toxic. Steve stated:

> I feel like a goldfish who has lived in a dirty bowl with dirty water my entire life. When I went to [another country, which Steve shared had more Black people], it's like somebody took me out of that [USA] environment, put me in a clean bowl with fresh, clean water. I had no idea those things existed. I could not live them in the United States. As much of a welcoming wonderful space [town in the west] is compared with a lot of other places in the country or even in [the west coast], it still has those same characteristics.

Given that Black masculinity in the USA is attributed as violent and threatening, particularly by white people (Brooms and Clark 2020), these experiences were becoming increasingly dangerous for Steve, and he was in the process of moving to that different country precisely to remove himself from the system of racialized gender – the dirty bowl with dirty water – that exists in the USA.

Dante, a South Asian trans man, had similar experiences growing up in predominantly white neighborhoods. He shared:

> I'm definitely not white, and yet in many ways I'm very white. I'm South Asian, but I grew up in a very white town, where there was maybe one other South Asian family [and] I think I saw one Black person once in town who went to our school. It's a very white neighborhood, and I didn't experience very much racial stuff from my other classmates. I was, you know . . . the

stereotype for me is that I'm very smart 'cause I'm Asian. In some ways, it's not a bad stereotype to have, and I was really smart, so it wasn't that I had to fight against that stereotype.

Dante's discussion of whiteness was not in relation to how he identifies or how others attribute a racialized identity to him, but about the ways he was allowed to participate in some aspects of white habitus as a person of South Asian descent in a predominantly white area. This was specifically in relation to being Asian, and arguably in growing up being perceived as feminine as well. Dante's experience is likely due to the myth of the model minority, which frames people of Asian descent as "living examples of advancement *in spite of* the persistent color line and *because of* their racial (often coded as cultural) differences" (Wu 2014:6, emphasis in original; see also Chou and Feagin 2008). In an extensive review of research about the model minority myth, Walton and Truong found:

> the overall societal impact of the [model minority myth] is that it presents a false assumption that people of Asian descent no longer experience racial disadvantage or discrimination, thus reinforcing existing racist structures and contributing to their endurance and adaptability across time. (2023:408)

While Dante felt that the myth of the model minority allowed him to fit in with his white peers and teachers, he was still perceived as a racial other. In other words, this acceptance into whiteness was conditional, temporary, and dependent upon him living up to the model minority stereotype.

Marisol had a similar conditional acceptance into whiteness. In addition, Marisol was born outside the USA and was not an American citizen. Marisol (straight Latinx trans woman) shared:

> I mean, it's hard, because I think a lot of people read me as a woman, but not a lot of people read me as Latinx. They either

Whiteness

83

read me as white passing or ambiguous, unless I am the person who says, "Oh, yeah, I'm from Mexico, born in Mexico, raised in the culture, I'm Latinx." Then it's, like, "What is Latinx?" I just say "Latina." I think that a lot of the time my race is forgotten in the work that I do, or forgotten in the aspects of my gender identity, or in the queer umbrella spectrum as a whole. I also think that race is the one thing that people do notice, because they have these questions. I have been approached by several people who have felt the need to ask me for clarification on my race, and insinuate that because they have a doctorate or whatever that they are medically licensed to do so. Or people who don't see my race unless I bring it up, or I start speaking in my native tongue. I think it's difficult because it's like you can't . . . there is no middle ground. It's just like you're pulled in one direction as not being in a race. Then in a direction as being in a race, but not knowing where it is. I think it's been difficult trying to keep the two together, because it's always . . . either it's my trans identity or it's my race identity in this area. People still don't understand that those things exist, can coexist together . . . I think I'm very ambiguous in both senses, because I pass, which is a term I hate to use, but I pass in cis spaces most of the time, and I blend in into white spaces.

For Marisol, she feels ambiguous because others perceive her race in ways that do not align with her self-understanding, and that this is particularly true in spaces where she is out as trans; her racial identity is erased in part at the expense of her trans identity being recognized. In addition, when she was perceived as white, it provided temporary attributions of USA national belonging that were constantly at risk of being denied. Similar to some people of color who are perceived as white, Marisol would occasionally benefit from white privilege, and yet this inclusion in the fold of whiteness was fleeting. Speaking Spanish or addressing where she was born would quickly shift others' perceptions of her away from whiteness and increase

84   Transgender Intersections

her experiences of racism. As Sowards notes, the "power of passing as white is also in flux and contingent upon moments and contexts of identification" (2021:45). While Marisol did not identify as white, she recognized situations in which this was happening and the ramifications it had for her interactions with others.

Unlike Marisol, Scout's (multiracial queer transsexual man) Latino identity was racialized as Brown. However, although he was an American citizen, his Americanness was questioned by others, particularly white people, in interaction because of the ways he was racialized (as discussed in Chapter 3). Scout shared his experiences of being in predominantly white spaces:

> As a trans person of color, I feel like white trans people are often my biggest oppressors, because they want to assimilate into being accepted by whiteness. And if they can assimilate like that, people forget about them being trans. I also find that white trans people who have completed physical transition, in ways where they pass . . . like, while changing in a locker room, often assimilate to my oppressors in the most loud ways. So that's really interesting to watch that climb into . . . climb out of being part of the targeted group into being part of those targeting, and I'm seen as a Brown person pretty much at every turn . . . People who want to socially climb at the cost of the most marginalized are often the most violent.

Scout's experience was in relation to white trans people not just perpetuating white normativity, but white normativity in intersection with cisnormativity and heteronormativity while upholding rigid racialized gender norms, particularly around bodies. Scout's narrative also relates to what Jesperson calls "settler *trans*nationalism": "certain trans bodies 'pass' into the U.S. body politics, not just through gender, but through investment in, and allegiance to, the nation" (2022:33, emphasis in original). As discussed in Chapter 3, Scout's racialization as

Whiteness 85

Brown marked him not only as non-white but also as an outsider to American nationality defined in relation to whiteness. Whiteness and nationalism are intimately interconnected, where being considered American is about inhabiting and maintaining white dominance. In other words, since normative citizenship is constructed as white, cisgender, heterosexual, and able-bodied, among other dominant categories, trans people whose habitus includes other socially normative categories more easily belong or are accepted as belonging (Aizura 2006; Wentling 2020).

While Scout perceived white trans people as often his "biggest oppressors," Leela, an Indian cis woman who was engaged to Kyle (white trans man), shared similar feelings about white people more broadly, saying "I was very angry at white people." However, Leela also noted that her partner, Kyle, was engaged in work around antiracism, which was incredibly important to Leela and to their relationship. She shared:

> I'm very lucky in that Kyle is an extreme champion of race issues. And sometimes I have gotten frustrated with my white peers or white friends, because there's this tendency to be like, "I'm an ally, kumbaya." He's not that person. He teaches courses on race. He's always trying to unravel privilege and get people to really look at it. And I think the reason he's so good at it is the position he was in in his life. I would argue that trans people are really like at the bottom of the pyramid. I guess the true bottom of the social power pyramid being a Black trans MTF person, I guess. So, you know, he's a little above, because then he always talks about how much his life shifted as soon as he became a white man. So he is incredibly sensitive and open and understanding of his position of power in this relationship and all kinds of things.

Leela's analysis addressed how she felt her trans partner had a position of power through his whiteness, including in relation

86   Transgender Intersections

to her, now that he was a white man. In a parallel way, she addressed her own cis privilege, and both cis and white privilege intersected within their relationship dynamics.

Another experience for Black, Indigenous, and other trans people of color involved the ways whiteness shaped people's perceptions about 2SLGBTQIA+ (Two-Spirit, lesbian, gay, bisexual, transgender, queer, intersex, asexual, and more) identities. For some trans participants of color, people in their communities of color perceived trans, as well as queer, identities as white phenomena, similar to the findings of Alimahomed (2010). While participants in this research recognized this was not true, it created additional challenges for them. Dante commented:

> And then there's the cultural thing of how my family acts with me being trans. It's not completely unlike the way that some white families react to it, but my family often feels like, "What has this white country done to you? It's a white thing, all this gay, trans stuff." It's silly, but it's how some people look at it.

In addition to these challenges of being acknowledged within communities of color, Dante, Steve, and other BIPOC participants experienced exclusion from white normative trans and 2SLGBTQIA+ spaces. As Josie and Katrice shared in Chapter 2, the exclusion of BIPOC trans people by white trans people included both overt and covert interactions.

White People Resisting or Acknowledging Whiteness

While there were no BIPOC trans people in this research who actively denied their own racial identities, the ways that their racial identities related to systems of power, or that whiteness is the dominant racial category, this denial was, unfortunately but expectedly, a relatively common experience for white trans people, as it was for April. The white trans people we interviewed could typically discuss intersections with other marginalized categories such as being poor, disabled, or queer, but they often stated that race was less or not at all significant in their lives. In some of these cases, they seemed unable or unwilling to grapple with how whiteness as a dominant and privileged identity shaped their lives. For instance, Craig (white working-class trans man) discussed how shifting from middle to working class and the change in social circles altered his definitions of masculinity. In his case, (white) working-class masculinity entailed meanings of family connection, protection of (white) women, and a willingness to fight. For instance, he noted, "you protect your family, you respect your mother . . . these kinds of roles are important." However, Craig did not acknowledge how his experience of working-class culture was shaped specifically through whiteness. It is important to analyze the ways that whiteness is tied to gender, social class, and sexuality, even though it may not be directly acknowledged by those maintaining a perceived white identity as they transition (see Lewis 2004).

For some white trans participants, questions about their racial identity were met with relative brevity compared to the analyses of trans BIPOC. Lee (white, queer, pansexual FTM) acknowledged having white privilege but didn't have much to say about it. He shared, "I don't really feel too much connection to my whiteness." This is another way white trans people implicitly resisted whiteness, and it was demonstrated by a number of white trans participants who recognized their racial identity as a demographic marker and even recognized systemic racism, but had not fully considered the way whiteness shaped their daily interactions. This can be a common experience of white people, as the experience of a privileged category is often structured so as to be normative and otherwise unmarked (Ahmed 2007; Brekhus 1998).

Some ways white trans people came to engage with their whiteness were through a discovery of their ancestry/heritage

88   Transgender Intersections

and newer engagement with what Torkelson and Hartmann (2020) refer to as racialized ethnicities. Ata (white, queer nonbinary femme) shared her shift in discovering her ethnic identity:

> [It's] been sort of a fun, newer thing in my life, is just like really hitting those Celtic roots hard to practice spirituality and explore pagan rituals and beliefs, and do some just like classic, earthy, witchy shit. A lot of it is coming from Ireland and Wales. Getting in touch with my ancestry and those traditions has been helpful to me, because I think, as white people, the constructive whiteness and the actual erasure of, like, Old World ethnic identities and immigrant stories has been part of white supremacy and the construction thereof. I think, if everyone traced their roots back a little bit and tried to find some touchstone in their family history, I think that would really help the sort of identity crisis that white people feel in this country particularly.

What is interesting with Ata is her acknowledgement of holding a white identity while simultaneously distancing herself from the construction of whiteness as related to systems of power. During the course of the interview, Ata indicated that she wanted to challenge white supremacy; however, claiming this type of symbolic ethnicity does not dismantle white supremacy, but rather allows for individual distancing from responsibility around whiteness: "those who cling to these cultural identities often opt into a white cultural polity when advantageous" (Matias and Boucher 2023:69).

White trans folks with some awareness of race and racialization often discussed the ways other white people resisted their attempts to address whiteness. The white people around them had often denied or minimized whiteness, even while discussing the significance of race for people of color. For instance, Aurora, a white, twenty-one-year-old genderqueer individual,

Whiteness

commented about silencing responses from others when they/ fae wanted to discuss race, saying:

> It's also interesting 'cause I wanna have a lot of conversations about race, and since that conference, and since having those white caucus spaces to talk about white allyship and performativity bullshit that happens a lot, I wanted to bring some of those conversations back to [university], and I feel I've gotten ignored or a pushback from people on that, because they're like, "No, you just talk about your queer shit" is kind of what I get from some folks and/or just ignored and like, "Oh, maybe we can do that another time or something," because I feel specifically in [town], and [state on the west coast] just in general, as a state it's very "all lives mattery," and I just don't buy into that. And so I'm like, let's have these conversations, 'cause I feel like I definitely had a conversation with my mom once about how, why didn't we ever talk about race when we were growing up and stuff like that, and she was like, "Well, I didn't want to perpetuate racism by talking about it." And I'm like, "Well, okay, but I feel like not talking about it is what perpetuates it because then we don't have actual knowledge or language to use to combat it, and also we live in a racist system." We're always moving towards racism unless we walk away from it, move away from it.

Similar to some other white trans participants, Aurora highlighted how growing up in white normative neighborhoods and spaces contributed to a denial of whiteness as a racial experience. Aurora was feeling motivated to discuss and address whiteness and racism with other white people, though, and faer experiences demonstrated other white people's resistance to that. Aurora's motivation extended beyond discourse to a desire to figure out ways white (trans and nonbinary) people can take action to resist white supremacy. For instance, they were referencing Beverly Daniel Tatum's moving walkway when Aurora stated "we're always moving towards racism unless we walk away from it, move away from it." Tatum describes this moving walkway:

> I sometimes visualize the ongoing cycle of racism as a moving walkway at the airport. Active racist behavior is equivalent to walking fast on the conveyor belt. The person engaged in active racist behavior has identified with the ideology of White supremacy and is moving with it. Passive racist behavior is equivalent to standing still on the walkway. No overt effort is being made, but the conveyor belt moves the bystanders along to the same destination as those who are actively walking. Some of the bystanders may feel the motion of the conveyor belt, see the active racists ahead of them, and choose to turn around, unwilling to go to the same destination as the White supremacists. But unless they are walking actively in the opposite direction at a speed faster than the conveyor belt – unless they are actively antiracist – they will find themselves carried along with the others. (2003:28)

Aurora's experience demonstrates the ways fae understood themself as part of a white supremist system, the ways they benefited from white supremacy, and the hope that faer actions might work to change the system. For Aurora and others who experienced similar dynamics, it was often a change that prompted awareness and insight into whiteness. These changes included the process of transitioning, connecting with other trans people, attending higher education, attending an event such as a conference, or moving to a less racially white area than where they had grown up. When attempting to bring this awareness and dialogue back to white communities, it was met with silencing rhetoric more often than not. This is what Lipsitz (2006) refers to as part of the investment white people engage in to maintain white normativity.

Whiteness 91

Lucas (white, queer, working-class FTM) shared some similar feelings in wanting to challenge white supremacy. He was attempting to address his whiteness, particularly in relation to conversations with his friends of color:

> The conversation that I have in my head a lot or that I struggle with is just ... I've been trying to do a lot of reading about whiteness and race and how to be a good accomplice. Some of the emotions that I come up against sometimes is just like, "Well, I'm a minority, too, and I have a lot of struggles being a trans person and feeling invisible as a trans person." I struggle with how to hold space for that and, also, not put that on to my friends of color. Because, what I find really frustrating is sometimes people get into these oppression Olympics ... A big question that was raised for me when I came out here and started living this way was, "Well, how do I leverage the white privilege that I have and this cis-passing privilege that I have to help my friends out?" Also, it's working on just putting down my own feelings of discomfort, maybe, around being white, definitely looking at a lot of white guilt and how to put that down and how to cede power. That's the phrase that I've really been thinking about a lot. That started happening when I started dating my girlfriend because I would think a lot about, "How do I empower this person? How do I cede power as a white cis-passing male to these people who are systematically oppressed?"

Lucas's experience of whiteness was intimately linked with his trans identity. In particular, his move to a predominantly white rural area on the west coast solidified his white, working-class masculine identity and the ways others now interacted with him. This was contentious for Lucas because his trans identity, and shared systematic oppression, was not visible to others. Simultaneously, he was recognizing that he might be able to use his white, working-class masculine privilege to challenge

92   Transgender Intersections

systems of inequity. While Lucas was considering how he might do all this, he struggled to find ways to put it into practice.

Charlie (white, queer, trans* man and veteran) talked about his awakening to his racial privilege as he transitioned. It is significant that trans experience can have the possibility of orienting a white trans person towards their whiteness. Charlie shared:

> And then becoming a man, suddenly in the spaces that I was a part of, it's like white men were – are – the worst, and suddenly I was becoming a white man, and I was like, oh, this is the way I take up space. This is the way, not only that my masculinity takes up space in a room, but suddenly my whiteness . . . I think as a woman and coming from the place that I came from, I didn't really realize the power that I had [in relation to my white identity], because I didn't think that I had power, and then suddenly, I don't know. It's hard to explain, but I was being made aware of both at the same time, and it was a lot to take in to deconstruct and be like, "Whoa, this is who I am authentically, and this is who essentially runs the world." I don't know. Who has the most power, who is in the top of all the governments? Basically, all the businesses, all the CEOs, white men.

Unlike many of our white trans participants, Charlie was actively experiencing how his gender was racialized and his race gendered, as well as the ways being a white man carried different meanings and experiences than being perceived as a white woman. Charlie's awareness grew in relation to both structural power and the white masculine privilege that he now held. As Charlie was interacting with others who affirmed his (white) masculine identity, he recognized that this was a racialized gender experience and that his perceived whiteness was interconnected with his masculinity. This was a newer experience for Charlie and, like Lucas, he was still working through what it meant in his daily life.

Whether resisting or acknowledging whiteness, many white trans participants experienced a change in racial awareness as they experienced a shift in their gender identities and/or when they connected with trans communities. Because whiteness shapes and interacts with gender, the shift in their experiences of racialized gender helped some white participants grapple with their race in ways that are arguably more productive than resisting their whiteness.

Whiteness and Settler Colonialism

Whiteness is intimately connected with settler colonialism. This became apparent in a number of ways, one of which included trans people's engagement with land projects. The "frontier" settler colonial ideology, such as in the geographic region of the rural western USA, is built from and perpetuates genocidal practices against Indigenous communities (Madley 2016). For participants in our research, this particularly included settler colonialism against Shasta, Takelma, Kurok, and Klamath peoples. One research project focused on this area, situated in Southern Oregon and Northern California, to examine trans experience in a particular rural context in detail.

In the formation of Oregon and California, like other states in the USA, settler colonial violence was a tactic explicitly encouraged by the government and those in power, for instance through encouraging white people to claim land through violence (Reed 2023; Risling Baldy 2013). These practices were built alongside and linked to white supremacy; Oregon, for example, also held explicit laws that prohibited Black people from owning land (Nokes, n.d.), and many rural towns in the western USA, including in Oregon and California,

94   Transgender Intersections

observed sundown laws (Loewen 2005). Sundown laws and practices prohibited non-white people from being in towns after "sundown," thus prohibiting them from residing in the area. Counties also supported Japanese American internment or concentration camps, including the Tule Lake internment camp in this region (Goulding 2019). Active white supremacist groups, such as the Ku Klux Klan, held town parades, and members, including those in national leadership positions within the KKK (Horowitz 1989), are still active today in this area (SPLC, n.d.). These traditions continue, and even in the supposedly "liberal areas," overtly violent acts of settler colonialism and racism are far too commonplace.

Complicating the dynamics of this region are numerous so-called "land projects," several of which center trans and queer lives. These land projects became popular during the 1970s–90s and have continued in many rural areas (Morgensen 2009; Schweighofer 2018). They invoke ideas of going "back-to-the-land" or homecoming (Morgensen 2009), and may have connections to environmental movements or philosophies, to radical movements such as radical lesbian feminism or the radical faeries, or other connections to social movements (Morgensen 2009; Schweighofer 2018). Morgensen argues: "Adapting back-to-the-land practices placed radical faeries in the historical trajectory of counterculturalists, naturists, homesteaders, and frontiersmen, whose practices of settlement included imperialist nostalgia for Native Americans" (2009:84). Land projects in this region are typically very rural, with people often moving from other, more populated areas to the land project either temporarily or permanently to engage in explicit community formation and alternative living.

Participants discussed two land projects that were more robustly active with trans inclusion in this region. One queer community stated their intention to "dismantle structures of oppression within and between us," and, according to some participants, the community was engaging in work to be trans

Whiteness 95

inclusive. Another project was centered on community among and between trans femme people. This community reached out to trans folks in urban spaces, encouraging them to come be part of the community for shorter or longer periods.

The relationships between the land projects and surrounding communities are complex. Lucas (white trans man) had originally moved from an urban area to join one of the land projects, and he discussed the ways that conservative white community members interacted with the predominantly white queer/trans land project members. Lucas shared:

> There's a pretty firm queer presence here ... There's a ... [queer land project]. They've been here for a long time, so people are used to queer folks around ... There's ... a transfemme-centered land project ... People know about that up there ... They kind of do, and they just don't want to see it, they don't want to have it in their face, but they don't bother us. They leave us alone essentially. There are really good connections that have been made with the close neighbors.

Lucas called these connections with neighbors "weird" because "there's [conservative political] signs all over the place," and "a pretty big contingent of neo-Nazis in this area. [Town] White Pride. It's the whole thing. You'll see that, [town initials]WP spray painted places." Although trans, and queer, identities are under ideological attack by many people in these communities, part of the ways in which these trans-inclusive land projects coexist with local conservative communities is through whiteness and settler colonialism. The predominant whiteness of the land projects creates racial "solidarity" with the broader white community and settler society even for trans-based and trans-inclusive land projects. This may at times also intersect with a social class solidarity. Furthermore, as Jesperson (2022:33) argues, "the rubric for trans passing in the U.S. is mediated by racialized and nationalist gender norms, through which white trans people, as settlers on stolen land, are afforded greater space for gender aberration." Lucas noticed the ways he and other white trans people were somewhat accepted, or more tolerated, in a white nationalist region (similar to Abelson's 2019 findings). White and settler privilege then becomes a significant factor of acceptance, to a point, of trans people in rural areas. While some white trans people wanted to distance themselves from racism and settler colonialism, they benefited from being attributed a white settler racial identity.

The white settler trans folks we interviewed often attempted to distinguish themselves from the more conservative or overtly racist white settler folks in the area. Lucas, like some other participants, struggled to incorporate his whiteness into or in relation to his trans identity in an overtly racist area, while simultaneously performing a rural white settler working-class masculinity that, as Abelson (2019) notes, is related to greater acceptance. It is particularly the act of claiming land and of being part of these land projects that aligns with white settler colonial ideals of "conquering the wilderness" (e.g., frontiersmanship) and living in supposed "harmony with nature," which is then linked to what Morgensen (2009:84) names as "nostalgia for Native Americans."

Intersectionality and Whiteness

If, as we argue, normative and privileged social positions are just as important to account for intersectionally as marginalized and oppressed ones, how do trans people account for whiteness? Unlike trans BIPOC who could talk about their experiences with race in relation to their gender as well as analyze whiteness on a systemic level, white trans people overwhelmingly resisted or struggled with understanding how their whiteness shaped their lives, let alone their gender. It is this difficulty that provides insight.

We began the chapter with the story of April, who shared her discomfort with the concept of whiteness and white privilege while simultaneously constructing a white habitus. While some white trans people were attempting to address race and whiteness more directly, there seemed to be two paths. One resulted in white trans people claiming alienation because they felt their experiences of marginalization were somehow in conflict with others' experiences of racial oppression. The other included white trans folks who, to varying degrees, understood the systematic nature of white supremacy but got stuck in not knowing how to really challenge it.

This further demonstrates the ways white supremacy and settler colonialism are so embedded in our daily lives. For white people particularly, it can be challenging to imagine a future without them. Since many of the white trans participants also recognized racial inequity in our society, how do we move towards social change, when change requires us to directly engage with whiteness and settler white supremacy? The white trans folks in our study did not yet have these answers for themselves.

5

Race and Gender Intersections with Social Class, Sexuality, Disability, and Nationality/ Citizenship

Race and gender have been intersectional priorities for many of the scholars and activists who have contributed to theorization on intersectionality (see Collins and Bilge 2020), and many have also examined intersections between these and other social categories. Social class has often been a significant focus of intersectional work, and categories such as disability, sexuality, nationality and citizenship, and more are also regularly analyzed through intersectional scholarship. In this chapter, we revisit the intersectional prism to examine some of these categories in more depth, focusing specifically on ways they intersect with race and gender in the lives of transgender people.

Social Class

Much early and continued work on intersectionality has focused on intersections between race, class, and gender (Collins 1993; Collins and Bilge 2020). Social class has been and continues to be a significant prism plane to investigate when it comes to understanding BIPOC lives, trans lives, and, at the intersection, the experiences of trans BIPOC. It is also important in understanding white trans people's classed experiences and what that can reveal about the ways classism is intertwined with white privilege and gender.

Joe (Black, nonbinary, pansexual) talked about class inequality and the ways political divisions prevent people from recognizing that "we could definitely make better strides and get to this place of everybody . . . having a piece of the pie, so to speak." This was a possibility through coalition building across differences and class solidarity. Joe stated:

> So if the [white] working-class people that we see out here on the TVs and stuff that are screaming all this hate and all stuff like that would wake up and realize that they, too, are being used, you know? Just so rich people can stay rich. If everybody would just wake up and be like, "Oh, wow! You know we, we're all being used. We need to come together and stop all this."

Lance (Assiniboine (Nakoda) working-class trans man) also felt like there were a lot of political tensions between BIPOC and white working-class people, and he was committed to building greater working-class solidarity. In particular, Lance shared why and how he engaged in building solidarity with white working-class cis men:

> And then I think the other piece is really building this interconnectedness to each other. Like actually going back to that basic, basic thing of, the relationship is the most important thing. And I know as a raised rural person that I can't just be like, "That guy's a fucking asshole." Well, that fucking asshole fixes all the cars. So, I gotta have a relationship with that guy, right? And you know, that's what my mind is on a lot, even at work where I'm like, you know, there's a guy there that is really hard for me to deal with. And every day I make the decision that it's a new day. And how do I go connect with that guy? Because if

> I don't bring him along, who's going to bring him along? It's like that commitment we have to have to each other, like if you see somebody struggling and everybody walks by that person, it doesn't do anything. That's not community, that's like, "Oh, there's the leper. We're just gonna leave the leper over there." Like one of the things I've learned about straight working-class guys is they usually feel like shit about themselves, right? So it's like, all it takes is some time to listen to them, and say a few things, right? So how do I make that decision even though I'm so annoyed by that guy, right? I sometimes think of it as setting a limit and then really showing that person that I'm on their side while they have the feelings about the limit that I set. How do I simultaneously be like "No, you don't get to do that, and I'm 100 percent on your side." This is not about you being bad or good. This is about, actually, things will go better if you don't do that.

Because of the racialized political divisions in the USA, Lance felt it was important to be strategic in building class-based relationships and challenging particular ideologies and stereotypes. Noticeable particularly to trans BIPOC were the ways white working-class and white working poor trans people were socially pitted against trans BIPOC, and how this division prevented collaborating towards social change. For trans BIPOC participants, many addressed the importance of building class solidarity across racialized lines, both within trans communities and in their other circles of influence, like Lance addressed.

Research often shows that BIPOC (Draut 2018) and trans people (Goldsen et al. 2022), even as separate categories, experience significant disparities in terms of social class, and trans BIPOC experience disproportionate oppression linked to social class (James et al. 2016). According to findings from the 2022 US Transgender Survey, "More than one-third (34%) of respondents were experiencing poverty," likely in part due to an 18 percent unemployment rate (James et al. 2024:21).

Social class also heavily factors in access to resources, such as health care, housing, and community. Josie (middle-class African American trans woman) spoke to the ways this was racialized, noting: "As I said before, we have to learn our own way, because we can't ever give up. We African Americans cannot afford [gender-affirming] surgery, cannot afford it. So we gotta figure out a way to make it work." Josie was specifically comparing the experiences of herself and other poor, working-class, and middle-class Black trans women with those of white trans women she knew who had greater access to class-based resources such as health care, housing, and so on.

In the USA, access to health care is often dependent on the type of job you hold, your income, and/or if you qualify for state-sponsored health care. In the latter situation, the health care available to trans people is dependent on the coverage or exclusions offered through a particular state's trans health policies. This has significant implications for trans people, particularly those in poverty. Several participants shared how a state's trans health policies factored into whether or not they relocated to that particular state.

When asked about their social class, many white trans participants asked questions about definitions of class status or seemed unclear about where they fit in terms of social class. A number of the white participants whose income placed them into working poor or working-class categories also indicated that they thought of themselves culturally as being middle class, even though they understood that economically they were not. For instance, ample minimum wage jobs do not provide opportunities for people to build financial security. However, a surplus of these types of jobs allowed for some trans people in rural areas to find employment. State-wide trans-inclusive policies also had an influence on employers, providing some guidelines around trans inclusion. As noted in the whiteness chapter, Jesperson (2022:33) argues that "the rubric for trans passing in the U.S. is mediated by racialized and nationalist gender norms, through which white trans people, as settlers on stolen land, are afforded greater space for gender aberration." One reason poor and working-class white trans people in rural areas may find acceptance around employment is due to their whiteness and alignment with settler colonialism.

Many of the trans participants in our rural study, even when employed, qualified for and were on state-funded health care systems. While trans-affirming medical policies alleviated some of the potential financial stress of being able to afford medically assisted transition procedures, these policies were not enough. They did not ensure that medical providers covered by the state's insurance were competent or trans-friendly, and participants shared their challenges in finding providers that were not hostile and were willing to work with them. This seemed particularly challenging for nonbinary folks. Those of a higher social class and with more financial resources were often able to shop around for a trans-friendly provider. Further complicating this was the availability of trans-friendly medical providers in some areas. Even being middle class did not mitigate the challenges of finding resources in these often poorer rural communities. The intersections of social class and the availability of trans-affirming services further factored into trans people's health and well-being.

Sexuality

Sexuality is another prism plane that is important in understanding the lives of transgender people. Many of our trans BIPOC participants were aware of the ways their attributed racialized gender was sexualized by others. The Asian American trans women shared their experiences of being attributed a desexualized racialized gender when they had been perceived as Asian American men (see Chong and Kim 2022) but an exotified racialized gender as Asian American women (see Azhar

Race and Gender Intersections . . .   103

et al. 2021), something we noted in Chapter 2. Elle (Chinese American, queer trans woman) spoke about her experience prior to coming out as transgender:

> In the previous year, my Mom actually asked if I was gay or not because I wasn't dating. And the mentality behind that was I just didn't want to get people involved. I was a very happy-go-lucky kid who just had lots and lots of dinner buddies, and I would carefully buy drinks for everyone. You need a ride to [the airport]? I'm your taxi driver. Kind of like the harmless Asian kid, but that you don't have to worry about being hit on. Now [after transitioning] I noticed a difference, because I can't really be friends with guys easily.

Elle was aware of the desexualized stereotype attributed to some Asian American men. While this is a harmful and limiting stereotype, it had also provided a sort of protective space for her prior to transition.

After transitioning, Elle relocated to a city on the west coast where most people only knew her as Elle. As she became friends with some people, she shared her story about being trans and she lost some friends. In our most recent interview, fourteen years later, Elle reflected back on the loss of these friendships: "I did lose another set of friends when I came out to them. Maybe they had some romantic interest or whatnot. I'm not really sure." Although Elle was out as a lesbian at this time, it's possible the hypersexualization attributed to being an Asian American woman contributed to others' interest in her prior to her coming out to them as trans.

Amber (a middle-class fourth generation Chinese American bisexual trans woman) specifically addressed the hypersexualization and objectification of Asian American women:

> During transition this pretty much all changed, and after transition instead of being the outcast, I'm the prized attention

getter, because you walk into a room and they're like, "Oh, here's the cute little Asian chick, I'm going to mack on her." . . . After surgery, you're feeling pretty confident, but you have to remember that now you are a sought after item, so instead of trying to get into groups, you're trying to get away from them.

Amber felt the need to "get away" from men who were sexualizing her, and she discussed how, as an Asian American woman, she was now a target of potential violence. This threat of violence was further complicated because of her trans status. These gendered, sexualized, and racialized attributions from others were something Topher (gay Asian cis man) also considered in relation to parenting a multiracial trans girl. In discussing safety, Topher said:

I also try to mitigate my own feelings about what I think she needs to do to be as safe as possible as a trans person. I think as I was trying to say earlier, her being Latina and Native American and so a trans woman of color, I know that distinctly they are subject to violence much more often, so that makes me nervous. It's one of those things, like, she's nine. I can't really explain that to her just yet, and I don't really know when or how I'm gonna explain it to her just yet. I think so many of the talks are different, and I've had to be very intentional about, how am I gonna navigate this talk? Like even the . . . trans-inclusive sex talk. I'm like, I don't know. It's just one of those things where. . . . Violence is definitely something I think about sometimes with regards to how to keep her safe and how to prepare her for the right partner or how to kind of talk her through it.

Topher was thus concerned about lessening the threat of violence for his daughter that BIPOC trans women experience in relation to sexuality and partnerships.

The meanings associated with certain racialized genders attributed to trans people also have an effect on their intimate

Race and Gender Intersections . . .

relationships and partners. Two white cis women who were partnered with Black trans men spoke about racialized interactions from others which intersected with others' perceptions of gender and sexuality. Both were perceived to be in interracial same gender relationships prior to their partner transitioning and perceived by others to be in interracial straight relationships after their partner had transitioned. Rebecca (white queer cisgender woman), partnered with Mike (Black trans man), noted:

> We would have some very negative experiences from people walking down the street. On the trains we get nasty looks. We once got spit on. We've been harassed and followed home and such. And we'd often talk about whether or not it's because it was two women [prior to transition], or if it was because of Black/white. And I don't think I have an answer, because they [the hostile actions from others] haven't changed that much from throughout the transition. And so what I had always seen as a homophobic thing may have been racist . . .

Rebecca had previously put the hostility they received from others down to their being perceived as a same gender couple, but as her partner transitioned and they were now perceived as straight, she noted that the discriminatory actions from others had continued, likely due to racism and the ways racism intersected with their perceived sexuality and genders.

Paige (white queer cisgender woman) had been partnered with Benjamin (Black trans man). Paige recounted that she and Benjamin had not experienced the same type of discriminatory acts from others prior to Benjamin transitioning, but she said that as he transitioned from being perceived as a Black woman to a Black man, she witnessed how others began to stereotype him as a threat and how the perceived changes also impacted their relationship:

Because he was Black, I also got to see this completely different side of ... you know? I'm white, I come from a small white town with mostly white people, and I had never really had to think about it before that. And because I also have primarily ... I have a lot of marginalized identities anyway, that I'd focus on them and then ignore the white privilege stuff. So, he really ... being in that relationship really forced me to see that kind of, "Oh fuck, people really are following you around stores now. Oh God, you just got racially profiled." I mean, the cop was like, "Oh, we're looking for someone who's 6'4" and Black, so we'll stop this 5'4" Black dude with dreads because obviously he's Black." It made it so real for me. I got to see people actually cross the street in front of him. I got to see people actually lock their doors when we would walk by. I got stared down by some people because we were holding hands. And I was told by someone I took one of the "good ones" away from her. This Black woman was like, "You took one of the good ones, and I can't forgive you for that." So it forced me to see my own privilege in this way that I had never seen before, and really made me think about it. And I think that I'm, I mean, I'm most grateful to him for that, because I got to see this transition ... It was interesting because when we were perceived as an inter-racial lesbian couple, it was actually OK. People left us alone more often than if we were seen as an interracial heterosexual couple. I mean, that was the most bizarre thing, because I was like, "What is it about the perception of him being a man that makes it so much different?"

Paige commented that she had felt people had mostly ignored her relationship with Benjamin prior to his transition, which might be attributed in part to the social invisibility of Black women in the USA. Yet, as he transitioned, she witnessed both significant changes in how others treated him, which led her to become more aware of her own whiteness, as well as changes in how others responded to them as a couple. For both

Rebecca and Paige, sexuality, gender, and race intersected, and shifts for their partner in gender had racialized and sexualized consequences.

The ways gender was racialized and sexualized were evident to Bazil (working-class queer Black and Iroquois trans man), who shared how others both hypersexualized and desexualized his racialized gender, sometimes in ways that aligned with how he felt about himself but also in ways that were constraining and harmful. Bazil shared:

> I was hanging out with people who boxed me in. They were totally cool with me being a man, but they would box me in so hard core into that. I was dating someone for two years, and she boxed me into this really traditional. . . . And it has to do a lot with race too, cause she was white, and boxed me into this Black guy to her, and really traditional, I guess you could say. But I think I'm more fluid than this . . . At first I thought I was fine with it, but then, just as any other label, there's the same amount of assumptions that go along with it.

In Chapter 2, we highlighted Dexter's experiences of being stereotyped in a hypersexualized racialized Latino masculine role, how he felt playful with this attribution at times but also concerned about how being constrained in this way might affect his ability to be himself with future partners. Similar to Dexter, Bazil felt stereotyped and somewhat conflicted with this particular hypersexualized racialized Black masculinity. Bazil felt affirmed by others in his gender as a Black man, but his masculine expression did not align with cultural stereotypes of particular types of hypersexualized Black masculinity.

Bazil also spoke about the ways he experienced desexualization in white queer communities. For example, he shared a story about performing as a drag king for a predominantly white queer audience:

> I think the first time I noticed it was at a drag show . . . I did a
> performance with someone . . . and I noticed, no matter what,
> it seems like when we did characters of color, we didn't get
> any response except from other people of color. It's not like all
> trans people have faux hawks or shaved heads. We were just
> not hot; I guess a trans guy can't have an Afro. And all the drag
> troupes, like the [drag king troupe name], I have friends who
> are in the [troupe name], and they have all white people. How
> does that happen? And one day I was like, "Why do you have all
> white people in your troupe?" She was just like, "Oh, we used
> to have this guy." Oh, you used to have your token and now
> you don't.

In contrast to the hypersexualization he experienced from his
white girlfriend and some of his friends, he felt his Black masculinity was not desirable in drag king spaces as it did not meet
the white queer masculine aesthetic expected of drag kings.
These collective experiences left Bazil feeling uncertain about
how to proceed with new relationships and with whom, saying
that because of many of these sexualized stereotypes, "I really
don't like dating that much."

Chance (working-class fluid Black trans guy) was also struggling with his new dating world. He felt sexual desire for cis
straight women but was unsure how to go about dating since
he felt that his body did not fully align with his gender. At
the time, he had talked with some other trans men of color
who had attended trans conferences where there were spaces
for Significant Others, Friends, Family, and Allies (SOFFAs).
Part of Chance's discussion addressed white cis women who
attended these spaces:

> I haven't had my first date with a straight woman, and that's
> because I said now that's a whole lot I have to tell them, so I'm
> still kinda with this juggling ball. Like, who really likes me? And
> I hear the SOFFAs women, most of them are white, not that I

have any prejudice, you know, towards any white women . . . but I don't know any SOFFA women that date trans guys, I haven't met any, so my dating is very, I don't know, man. But you know again when I first started transitioning I seen a lot of trans guys and they dated, they was dating men. I never knew that was an option, 'cause I love women. So I found myself, because of my sexual needs, I've been sleeping with guys. I can't see myself dating guys; I've just been sexually with them. And how do I feel about that? Well, I get to have a nut. You know, maybe it's the hormones that's making me sort of like, you know, fuck it, I gotta get off. So my dating is really turning now, and I haven't found, as far as who I am, far as in the dating, or haven't found how to connect with women that like trans guys. I don't know how to seek them out, I just don't know . . . You meet a lot of trans guys, persons of color, and that's just in the GLBT community too, but it's more lesbians if they're out today . . . Black [people] don't want to date trans guys. I don't think they know we're here.

Chance struggled with finding Black women who might be interested in dating him, particularly because he found 2SLGBTQIA+ communities to be predominantly white and found Black communities to be mostly cisnormative. Chance found a way to meet his sexual needs, although he was clear that he was not interested in relationships with men.

Several trans men talked about dating or having sexual relationships with cis men. For Scout, this was complicated by being Brown and later disabled. Scout noted that in the city where he lives, there were very few Brown men in the gay bars he frequented: "It's really in my face that I'm the only Brown one at [queer] event[s]. That I'm the only Brown one in the gay bar. I see maybe two or three other people, that's it." In our more recent interview, sixteen years later, Scout, who is married and polyamorous, talked about a queer event he and his husband attended:

> Nobody wanted to fuck the fat Brown trans disabled guy; they want to fuck my husband. You know, he's trans, he's white, he's able enough bodied. He's got the nicest legs you've ever seen, and he's fairly slim . . . and they all tried to bang him, and they all would give him time and space and centering and a lot, and at the cost of my inclusion. Like they would literally sleep with him, and then physically block me out of a conversation when I'm standing next to him. Wow!

In contrast to Dexter's experience of an exoticizing of his "Latinoness," Scout experienced a desexualization, particularly in white queer spaces. This may have had to do with numerous factors, including Scout living in a predominantly white city while Dexter lived in a city in the southwest with a greater Latinx population. Scout's desexualization was further exacerbated as his disability became more visible to others (Shakespeare, Gillespie-Sells, and Davies 1996).

Disability

Disability is a significant intersectional prism plane to incorporate when discussing the lives of trans people. Trans people are more likely than cis people to be disabled; Smith-Johnson (2022) found trans people were nearly twice as likely as cis people to have a disability. The number of trans people with a disability also increases with age (see also James et al. 2016). Further, trans people, and particularly trans BIPOC, experience high levels of discrimination, violence and threats of violence, microaggressions, and chronic stress, all of which can potentially contribute to disability and/or exacerbate discrimination related to disability.

Joe (Black nonbinary pansexual) shared some of their challenges. Across seventeen years between interviews, many of Joe's identities shifted: from not being disabled to being

Race and Gender Intersections . . .   111

disabled, from being a trans man to being nonbinary, from being gay to pansexual, and from being Christian to non-Christian. The shift in disability was significant for them; they/hym/syr felt that their interactions with others had changed, noting:

> A lot of communities, especially gay men, I think they're not really interested in always dealing . . . with people with disabilities. Because for them, for some reason it brings about a thing about death. Sickness and illness, and people don't always want to deal with those things. You know, they can deal with it from a far off place, but to deal with it right up in your face, you know, all the time, makes it kind of hard for them. So it kind of puts a pressure on the person with a disability to always be happy, you know, around these people. Even when you're not, and when you're not happy, because, like . . . last month or a couple of months, I've been going through a lot of physical issues, so it's hard to remain happy.

While Joe felt they had friends and community, they struggled to participate and find connection in broader trans and BIPOC community activities that were often inaccessible and exclusionary.

Scout (multiracial queer transsexual man) addressed the compounding structural marginalization he continually experienced. In the fifteen years between interviews, Scout experienced a life-changing event that left him with significant pain and mobility challenges. Like Joe, he faced challenges finding community that not only addressed his multiple marginalized identities, but also accommodated his physical needs. For instance, he mentioned finding some community events around some of his identities that turned out to be inaccessible. In addition, he would find community that created accessible spaces but was white normative and exclusionary in relation to him being Brown. In both frustration and empowerment, he

112   Transgender Intersections

shared: "I'm fucking forty, like every day is an active revolution by literally existing, and so that kind of feels powerful and like a 'fuck you' to the system." Isolation was significant for some of our disabled participants, which was clearly compounded for some of our disabled BIPOC participants such as Scout. It demonstrates the need for intersectional and inclusive trans communities that are actively working towards creating accessible spaces for multiply marginalized trans populations, including disabled people.

Nationality/Citizenship

A discussion of intersections with the prism plane of nationality and citizenship in the USA cannot proceed without a recognition of the current political and social discourse around the normative cultural constructs of "American." Many people today espouse white nationalist, transphobic, homophobic, and ableist rhetoric. In the USA, and arguably elsewhere in parts of the Global North and Global South, normative citizenship is constructed as white, cisgender, heterosexual, and able-bodied (Aizura 2006; Wentling 2020). Wentling further argues that "the logics of citizenship rely on binary sex/gender governing systems" (2020:1654). What happens, then, when trans people disrupt these systems through their own embodiments and changes in identifiers associated with nationality?

In Chapter 3, we outlined the ways some multiracial trans people experienced a shift from being perceived as white to Brown, and how that Brown identity was simultaneously defined as non-American; their nationality and citizenship were called into question by others in interaction. This shift from assumed American citizen to suspected non-citizen further demonstrates the normative cultural construction of the stereotype of what an American is supposed to be. It was not only embodied changes that shifted the cultural identities attributed by others to trans people; legal identification and perceived mismatches revealed cultural scripts around cisnormativity and whiteness. This highlights what Spade analyzes, particularly that:

> Identity documentation problems often occur for trans people when an agency, institution, or organization that keeps data about people and/or produces identity documents (e.g., driver's licenses, birth certificates, passports, public benefits cards, immigration documents) has incorrect or outdated information or information that conflicts with that of another agency, institution, or organization. (2015:78–9)

Marisol (Latinx, straight, trans woman) discussed her struggles in changing identity documentation as she went through the process of applying for a green card:

> When I had a visa, and my mom and I were applying to get green cards, I hadn't changed my name, and I wanted to change my name. That was a whole battle of my mom not wanting me to change my name, or being supportive and thinking that I could do it. Having to go through different mediums with the lawyer that we were with to get my name changed before we submitted the green card application. I had to change my name and give the name change documents to the lawyer so he could send it to Immigration, Immigration could process the application with my legal name change, so that on the green card it says my legal name as it is now. Previous, before that, I didn't have my name changed on my visa, because that didn't feel like an option. It was surprising that they did approve my name change, it was just difficult to get that process going . . . Because I tried to get my gender marker changed at the same time with supportive documentation, just from having a letter from a mental health therapist. That wasn't approved, I think because they wanted medical – like, they wanted [gender-affirming]

surgery before they would approve changing the gender marker on my immigration status and papers.

Marisol had felt in limbo and in potential danger with her identification marking her as a gender that did not align with her identity or with how others perceived her.

Marisol, who was twenty-three years old, also hoped that restaurants and bars, particularly those that advertised as 2SLGBTQIA+ or trans-friendly, might better train staff to not confuse identification with conflicting gender markers with fake identification:

> I don't want to say, "We're trans-friendly, we got a sticker," but you're really thinking of gender markers on ID, on identification. I think bars could have a training on that, and be, "is this ID fake, or is this not?" I think also when it comes to being in, not even bars, but restaurants, too, anywhere that serves alcohol, to have the training.

Although the state where Marisol lived allowed individuals to change their gender marker on their driver's licenses without "evidence," doing so would place Marisol in a situation where forms of identification did not match, because she had not been able to change her marker on her green card.

Even white, able-bodied trans people contested normative cultural scripts around citizenship, predominantly through the use of an X identity marker on their driver's license. Some states in the USA allow for individuals to select X (nonbinary or simply not F or M), F (female), or M (male) on their driver's license. While this creates space for legal nonbinary gender identification, this shift is not consistently reflected in other state-controlled documentation. For instance, one white participant who had changed their driver's license to X shared their experience of being denied a state license to purchase a gun because of their X identification. The paperwork for the license required them to select either M or F. They selected the marker that matched their birth certificate and past driver's license, but they were then denied the gun license because their "gender markers did not match," even though an X gender marker was not an option on the paperwork. Prior to changing their driver's license gender marker to X, they had never been denied a gun license. Although they shared that they attempted to discuss this discrepancy with state officials, they were told "nothing could be done." In essence, they became an unknowable citizen to the state.

While some participants experienced challenges in government recognition, for some trans BIPOC, their recognition by others as holding particular racialized gender markers had them question their own belonging within the borders of "American." Aizura found a "particular narrative of (trans) sexual citizenship that figures transgression as a necessary but momentary lapse on the way to a proper embodied belonging, a proper home and full inclusion" (2006:293). This belonging was not only about aligning with cisheteronormative gender, but how this was rooted in whiteness.

Over the years between the initial and follow-up interviews, two middle-class BIPOC participants shared that they had either moved or were in the process of moving to other countries. In part, this had to do with their racialized genders and the hostility and oppression they experienced in the USA. The type of hostility they experienced had shifted with their gender transition and the racialized gender markers ascribed to them. In Chapter 2, we addressed some of the consequences for trans people of moving to more socially visible racialized gender categories. The racialized gender meanings attributed to them by others were rooted in existing white cisheteronormative cultural narratives, but the shift of these experiences took their toll. A third participant who was middle class, trans feminine, and Asian American shared how she was ready to leave the USA if things got worse politically for her. In these three cases,

116   Transgender Intersections

they had the financial resources to leave and were also not bound to stay due to family or friend connections. While all three were American citizens and thought of themselves as American, the increasing white supremacist rhetoric around what it means to be American and how that excluded them was experienced as traumatic. These experiences of trans people reveal the ways "American" identity has been and continues to be framed as white, heterosexual, and cisgender. This social exclusion and marginalization in turn limit their participation as full citizens in society.

The Prism of Intersectionality

While race and gender have been central categories for much intersectional scholarship, part of the framework of intersectionality requires us to continue to ask which social categories contribute to systems of power and oppression and to incorporate those into our analysis. Our intersectional prism can turn and shift for us to bring particular categories to the forefront, and a strong intersectional analysis will require that, even if one or more categories are at the forefront, we are also considering the other prism planes of intersectionality as they mutually influence each other. As outlined in the intersectional model in Chapter 1, each plane is constructed beyond binary concepts, linking social positions within institutional and structural power to offer a richer analytical tool. Trans people's experiences and lives demonstrate the ways all people experience gender as racialized and race as gendered and how analyzing race and gender in relation to other planes of intersectionality reveals the complexity of lived experiences. Each plane of analysis thus provides further insight into the lives of trans people. If we seek to make trans lives better, we always need to explore how an intersectional perspective can help us better address inequities and calls to action.

6

Intersectional Trans Futures

Fourteen years prior, Amber and I sat in her basement with three other Asian American trans women during a group interview that she helped organize. Today, we connect via video conferencing technology, each sitting in our own home offices. Amber, a middle-class, fourth generation Chinese American bisexual trans woman, is now forty-eight years old. She's married, and she has remained in the tech industry. Fourteen years ago, Amber had been struggling because others in the tech industry did not value her ideas and contributions, in particular in relation to the shift in how others perceived her as belonging in the tech field prior to transition but not belonging as an Asian American woman, which we discussed in Chapter 2. As we talk, I ask about her experiences in the tech field today. She shares:

> I would say that the problem is a perennial problem. It was always there, it is, it always existed. I've just found myself to begin to have that problem [after I transitioned]. Then I figured out how to use the system to fight the problem. I still run into the problem. I just know how to avoid certain situations. It's just better tools, more wisdom, time. More patience, I think . . .

118   Transgender Intersections

> I think before [I transitioned] I would say things and get results. Now I have to literally warm people up, say things, keep them interested, and then I get results. And then I have to remind them that I was the one that gave them the results. So these are the new tools I picked up in the past decade and some and change. Oh, and you have to do this while staying humble. It's really, it's an art, and it's such an art.

While this was clearly a gendered problem, Amber felt that it was about more than gender and that others did not experience challenges in the same racialized gender ways that she did. She shared:

> I have a transgender friend who is white. She does not have the same problems as me, who is a person of color. We're both of a similar age. We're both, you know, in the same sort of tech space; but I feel that she doesn't get splash damage from certain things, whereas I do . . . But if you are a transgender person of lighter skin, shall we say, you can kind of go unnoticed in certain circles; whereas people who are transgender and who are not white, you get some weird splash damage from all other stuff going on. So I feel like it compounds . . . I mean, I just think it's multi-level anxiety.
>
> Imagine you're driving a car, right? You're just driving down the road. What do you have to worry about in terms of crashing? Well, usually the thing in front of you and people behind you. Occasionally, it's the things on the side, like somebody's trying to change lanes or merge onto the road. But you've never asked the question, "Is the ground going to fall out below me?" No, you've never asked that. You've never asked the question of like, "Am I getting dive bombed?" No, no, there are two totally different directions that you don't have to worry about. But let's say you were a person that has a convertible, now you're worried about birds crapping on you. That's a vector of attack that you did not know. For me, that's kind of like how

intersectionality kind of works. It's just like, man, you have so many more weak points, because all the weird stuff can happen to you.

For Amber, holding multiple marginalized identities made one more of a target for attack and discrimination in ways that people with more privileged identities didn't recognize or anticipate. Further, that anticipation of attack – of the potential for violence and discrimination – is something she lived with regularly. As she states "it's the same thing as racism, like you just don't know the barrier is there until you bump into it." She also noted how being "heteronormative" meant her and her husband did not "get flack for our relationship" compared with queer couples they knew; she felt like she and her husband could "sympathize," but it was not in the realm of their experiences.

Amber shares how the current political climate and rhetoric "just kick my anxiety into overdrive. I think that I'm really worried about certain people that I know who are recently transitioned, or in transition, or something like that, or just experimenting." She was specifically referencing the current anti-trans political climate and anti-Asian violence in the USA. Beyond the high number of bills being put forth and passed, of significant concern for Amber and some other participants were the requests from government officials for the names and records of transgender people, particularly youth (Keith 2022; Turban, Kraschel, and Cohen 2021). As someone in the tech industry, Amber expressed particular concerns about trans vulnerability related to technology and politics:

I would say proceed with caution . . . It's so easy to leave a digital trail . . . Anything you use today, it's heavily scraped. And so, unfortunately, I never thought that transgender care would be in the center of public attention in the past two years. I would say that being very, very open on the internet is more

120   Transgender Intersections

problematic because you're just putting more data signals out
there. And until the political environment calms down a little
and people just start getting back to worrying about general
living, this is going to be problematic.

When I interviewed Amber fourteen years ago, we had connected because of her use of online forums, groups, and other
trans-related websites and resources. However, she had now
become much more concerned about online information
precisely because of what she perceived as a dangerous political climate. Amber's concern was twofold: she was worried
about the ways trans people in general were being targeted
as well as how trans BIPOC were at a greater risk because
of their racialized gendered identities. She also reflected on
how, fourteen years ago when we first spoke, trans people
were able to transition somewhat under the political radar.
While there were challenges in that, she reflected that there
seemed to be less fear among people she knew then than
today.

While Amber was concerned about the safety of trans
people, BIPOC, and trans BIPOC, like many of the trans
people in our research who have been out for several years, she
felt a certain responsibility to be the more vocal voice, to be a
"bridge builder":

> The interesting thing is, I would say, in the past year, year-and-
> a-half, I've been a little more open at work about being trans.
> And I think, and the reason for that, in my opinion, is that I
> feel I lead by example. It encourages other people to be more
> open about their identities, whatever it is. Even if they're just
> supportive, I think it's really important to be visible or to show
> support.

This was Amber's call to action, for those who had been out
as trans for some time and were structurally safer: we should

be the ones challenging what is happening politically, whether that's in our own spheres or more broadly.

The importance of intersectionality lies not only in how it helps us understand society, but also in how it helps us build a more equitable society through politics, social change, and activism. Addressing how race, gender, and other social categories shape experiences of politics and social action can help us create intersectional trans futures. Given political attacks on trans rights, as well as heightened social discourse in support of ongoing white supremacy, the intersections between trans identities and race are as critical as ever. How do these ongoing gendered and racialized processes impacting trans people shape our society? If race is central to understanding trans experience, what are the implications of understanding gendered racialization processes for promoting both antiracist and transgender activism? While white supremacist settler cissexism is certainly embedded in our current society, we suggest there is hope for social change as we work towards dismantling these systems and replacing them with something new.

Politics

We would like to return to Scout, who said "every day is an active revolution by literally existing, and so that kind of feels powerful and like a 'fuck you' to the system." Experiences of exclusion and threats of violence were at the core of our discussions around politics and trans experience. Participants in more recent interviews expressed higher levels of fear about the political discourse related to their identities in the USA and worldwide. Of particular concern was the increasing cissexist, racist, homophobic, misogynist, and ableist rhetoric from political figures and the general public, including via social media (Southern and Harmer 2019). Participants discussed how white nationalist and anti-trans rhetoric and legislation has increased, becoming much more overt (Atwood, Morgenroth, and Olson 2024; Hsu 2022; Mayne 2019). In discussing her experiences of being Asian American in the USA, Amber commented that it felt "like you're constantly under a microscope." Some trans people who have not disclosed their trans identity or experience to others might be able to remain somewhat invisible to increased surveillance. Trans people who cannot do this, and those who choose to be open about being trans, might be under greater surveillance. Because being BIPOC already entails greater surveillance, as discussed in earlier chapters, the trans BIPOC participants often felt that regardless of how normatively they expressed their gender, they remained under higher levels of threat, which increased exponentially at the intersections of their race and gender.

As a result, many participants engaged in cautionary behaviors, such as Amber being more careful about information she shared online. In addition, in my second interview with Steve (Black trans man), he shared:

> I don't travel to North Carolina, because I assume it's illegal for me to use the bathroom that is safest for everyone concerned, [the one] that I use. So, I won't even go there. . . . The trans blowback concerns me a lot.

This policy, that would either force him to use a women's bathroom in alignment with the law or to use a men's bathroom at the risk of being arrested if he was discovered to be trans, was a significant concern to Steve, particularly because he felt highly surveilled as a Black man. Because of this, he refused to travel to that location. Similarly, Dante, a Southeast Asian trans man, shared how, when he traveled for work, he had a stipulation in his contracts about safety around health emergencies related to discriminatory practices and laws that may allow providers to refuse care to trans people: "I do write things like, if there's a medical emergency, send an advocate with me, because,

Intersectional Trans Futures 123

because I'm [a trans man of color]. And I don't want to be there by myself." Topher (gay Asian cis man) is the parent of a multiracial trans girl, and he also discussed his concerns about travel within the USA:

> Before I had a kid, even though I'm gay and Asian, whenever I was job searching, I'd be like, "I'll go anywhere. I can make it work 'cause it's myself." Now that I have a kid and I'm like, "Okay, this is a multiracial, transgender child," when I start thinking about my next step or if I ever wanna relocate, it's a much smaller map of, "Oh, what states have protections and what states am I not gonna get fired?" and stuff like that. That's definitely affected some of those outlooks and philosophies. I have a friend who lives in Georgia. I was like, "I wanna visit you, but now I'm nervous to visit you." They're also gay so they're gonna be fine with [his transgender daughter], but it's also just going out and doing things and figuring out, what are the bathroom laws in different states? I travel a lot. I still travel a lot even with her, but it's very specific now, intentional.

The intersections around racialized gender left Amber, Steve, and Dante feeling at a greater threat of potential violence and discrimination, and Topher realized this was also true for his child. However, they all recognized that they had some economic privilege that allowed them to make somewhat safer choices in relation to potentially violent or harmful contexts.

This shift of trans people becoming more of a target by the state and being under greater surveillance by the public is already an experience more common for BIPOC in the USA. However, it had a new effect on many white trans people, since this tended not to be something they had experienced in the same way before. For some of the white trans participants, the rise in anti-trans bills and rhetoric resulted in a type of political awakening. This was particularly salient for Aria, a sixty-four-year-old white transgender woman. Aria told me

124 Transgender Intersections

that, prior to transition, she had identified as "a straight, white, male Republican," but her gender transition influenced how she was now experiencing her social and political world, and her changing political ideas had also had an impact on her sense of self:

> [A conservative politician] started my real conversion, and really started me payin' attention again to what was going on, 'cause I was, like I say, a pretty white male Republican . . . It was kinda before it started, and I started changing, even before [gender transition], as far as my politics. It started becoming evident to me that [conservative politician] was an idiot. [He] starts talking, and he says, "You're bringing your worst. . ." – what he says about Mexicans. I'm goin', fuck, pardon my French there. I see these people in our neighborhood doing the housecleaning for people. I see them doing the yards. I talk to a lot of them. I work with some of them, and they're all very polite. They all seem very family-oriented. They're religious. Very rarely are they impolite. I don't see who you're talkin' about, Mr. [conservative politician], number one, and I kinda note that. I start watching debates, and I see [him] using these tactics, he's labeling people with nasty labels, like little Marco. Bullshit like that. That's not a debate tactic that's worth anything in my mind. It apparently influenced a lot of people. Then, he does that thing about that [disabled] guy and loses me, right there. My son is disabled, and I see that, and I go, you lost me there, bud. I'm also a business person, and he claims to be a business person. My first reaction when I hear that, by the way, this is before I started this stuff here. My first reaction was, "Yes! A business person, and a Republican as president. That could be great." That's what I'm thinkin'. Take care of all regulations. Take care of all that, but then, he proves himself to be an idiot.

Aria told me about how attacks on various marginalized communities other than those she belonged to started to strike her

Intersectional Trans Futures 125

as inaccurate. She named attacks on non-white, immigrant, and disabled people as all places where Republicans "lost" her, and she told me how some of these personal political shifts then paved the way for her gender transition. Aria was in tears as she discussed the political climate in the USA:

> I started losing faith in everything the Republicans did for it. They were not the big city lights on the hill. They're a stinkin' bunch of corrupted, "I'll do anything to get shit passed that hurts a lot of people." I don't like that tax cut they passed, 'cause I think it'll hurt people in the long run. I don't like what they try to do with Obama Care. I think they should've tried to improve it. I like the idea of having free education through college for people who, you've got my politics there, can completely change. I think there should be . . . I'll put it this way, transgender people have been on our planet for the entire history of our planet. We are not new. We've been here, so have gay and lesbian, bisexual, so have genderqueer, asexual, intersex. We have been here. We're not new. We've been part of the family for the entire history of our planet. We're part of the family. We deserve the same respect, the same rights, and the same courtesies as every other person on the planet, and we shouldn't have to fight for them, and we shouldn't have to be singled out, and we shouldn't have to go to court to get them. I put that on my Facebook page, something to that effect . . . kind of like a brief of my reawakening, my transition so far.

Aria was afraid because her gender transition shifted her experiences and her vulnerabilities. Instead of being perceived as an older straight white cis man, she was now an older white trans woman, someone she realized was now also a target.

Similar to Aria, Kitty (white, pansexual, trans woman) shared her own realization about her and other trans people's political vulnerability:

126 Transgender Intersections

> I guess this latest election made me realize just how vulnerable we could be and how tenuous that [is]. You have the acceptance, you have the tolerance, but something that happened this last year with [conservative politician] being elected makes you realize how fragile that can be, how thin of a margin there is and how dependent it is on where you are.

These shifts in awareness were personal, and for many participants meant speeding up transition-related procedures or changes in identification or becoming less open about their trans status with others. Their goal was to decrease their social visibility, with the hope that it would decrease potential threats of violence. D (white, queer and trans) shared:

> I surprisingly had some people in my life that actually voted for this [conservative] administration and they seemed okay with everything that was going on. I've been terrified of how it's going to affect health care and my access to health care. Just being able to afford medications in general, hormones aside. I have other medications I have to take for my disability, and it's made me afraid that I'm not gonna have access to that. I try really hard not to watch the news and not to read the news, but [with] this current political climate and what's going on in the world, I feel like I need to be informed. It's been stressful.

In this case, D had relied on his whiteness to avoid politics, but his experience of being trans and having a disability in what he understood as a more hostile political climate shifted his vulnerabilities.

For others, this shift had them reflect on their political positions and consider personal relationships. Charlie (white, queer trans* man) spoke about his fears and his personal relationships with politically different neighbors:

> I'm like, oh my God, I can't believe this is the state of affairs, and I am appalled, and I also saw myself detaching, which then

Intersectional Trans Futures

127

makes me feel like I'm doing a really terrible job as a citizen. I'm trying to figure out, 'cause in times past, I've been like, "I have to know all of the news. Because I'm informed, that makes me a good citizen and a good neighbor," and now I'm just detaching myself and checking out in a way that I'm like, "Am I just a coward? Am I a chicken because I can't handle that everyday there's some new atrocity?" . . . I'm just like, this is not who I am. I'm not. This can't be my country. I feel very beyond upset. I don't even know, I'm in left field. I'm in outer space right now. I feel like with mentally with what's going on national politics-wise . . . I think also getting to know our neighbors, I've done . . . our neighbors, when we first moved in, we didn't feel, like, they didn't like us all that much, because it just seemed like they weren't very friendly. Now that time has gone on, we've developed an established rapport. One neighbor that I did some work for, she has a Confederate flag in her bedroom, and I'm like, "oh my God. I can't believe I did work for this person." I'm looking at a Confederate flag, and she knows that I'm trans, and I know that she is [politically conservative]. I know she's Republican, but we have a friendship, and we're developing a friendship that feels authentic in a way that I do think that even if we don't agree on our politics that we're getting to know one another, and learn where each other comes from. I do feel like there's been growth and compassion. Maybe not necessarily am I gonna change her opinion in the voting booth, but there is a way that we're connecting. I don't think she knew any trans people before me.

Charlie felt potentially threatened by white supremacy (e.g., through displays of the Confederate flag and conservative political signs) because he identifies white supremacy as anti-trans. What is interesting is that although white supremacy is linked to anti-trans meanings, Charlie is somewhat accepted by this neighbor and they develop a type of friendship that is mediated through their shared whiteness. Over time, he

128 Transgender Intersections

does not feel as threatened engaging in interactions with his neighbor as he did in the beginning, and yet he still wonders how he might build upon the relationship to potentially shift her understanding of (white) trans people. What may be less likely is his ability to shift her opinions around race and white supremacy.

Charlie held on to the hope that positive individual interactions, in some ways educating neighbors, friends, and family about trans identity, might help create social change. In this sense, Charlie and others were hoping to demystify trans experience and counter the anti-trans rhetoric and incorrect information about trans people that has been increasingly deployed. However, interactions such as these were often reliant on whiteness.

While some trans people felt that sharing their trans identity with others might improve relationships, others were concerned for their own safety. A threat of violence was a recurring concern to participants. However, it was not only about the threat of experiencing violence, but also about the ways that someone learning about your trans identity could potentially shift the type of relationship that previously existed and lead to exclusion or other harm. In part, this was because much information about trans people perpetuates certain stereotypes that are often difficult for individual trans people to shift. Some trans people wanted others to acknowledge their gender without a trans label; however, not sharing their trans status was perceived by others as being inauthentic or "fraudulent" (Brumbaugh-Johnson and Hull 2019). This became an authenticity teeter totter, where trans people were balancing having their authentic gender acknowledged and accepted with their feeling of others' expectations that they should be out about any personal transgender history. Brumbaugh-Johnson and Hull (2019:1158) note that "coming out as transgender is not merely an act of declaring one's gender identity to self and others. Rather, it is an ongoing and situational process of navigating

Intersectional Trans Futures 129

the social implications of one's gender identity and gendered behavior." Brandon (sixty-one-year-old white, bisexual man) reflected on this authenticity teeter totter in his discussions about not engaging in that ongoing coming out process:

> Once you let that genie out of the bottle, there's no way to put it back in. I was heading that direction. I was edging my way towards that [letting friends know I was trans], not saying I was gonna do it, but I was really gettin' closer to, "Well, I might wanna do this depending on if I can connect with some trans people and maybe some more people, and now they know, and a little more people." I'm really torn because when [conservative politician] took office and then, as I'm sure you know … first they went after the trans students in bathrooms in schools. Then it's the transgender people in the military. I've just heard recently about whatever they're trying to do with taking medical care away from … It's been unrelenting. My feeling was I'll just stay … I'm hidden. I'm safe at this point. I'll stay safe. I just wanna keep a real close eye on where things go, see if it becomes safer, but I'm really torn emotionally between that, wanting to stay safe and stay stealth as I've been for so many years, and the fact that I was heading down this path to coming out, because, like I said, I've become very aware now of the costs of being stealth. There's a cost in intimacy 'cause I have close friends that don't know that I'm transgender, and so there's this huge part of me that I can't share with my closest friends without explaining what I'm referring to and why. I'm quite torn, and I feel like the political climate stopped me from doing something that I wanna do with my life.

Brandon was able to avoid disclosing his trans experience to others, including friends, community members, and many health care providers, and in part this had to do with his working-class white masculinity in a predominantly white area. Even still, Brandon carried a sense of loss about not

130 Transgender Intersections

being able to be his whole self. If he told folks he was trans, he would lose control over how that information was shared and with whom. Living in a small rural town also meant he would not necessarily be able to remain anonymous. In the wake of increasing anti-trans rhetoric and legislation, he felt that coming out potentially jeopardized his safety and his existing social support.

This shift in political awareness and increased vulnerability led some trans people to consider leaving the USA. Like Steve and some of the other trans BIPOC who moved or were considering moving outside the USA, some of the white trans participants shared similar thoughts because trans people, in general, were being targeted. Sky (white, queer, trans masculine) shared his reflections:

> [I] still have moments of it, where I don't know how long I can stay in the United States if it continues moving in the direction that it's moving. In my heart of hearts, I know that we're not going to be going down this road forever. I think it's a global awakening, hopefully, that's happening ... Politically, I feel really threatened in a way that I've never felt before. That, too, is adding to my want for studying more social justice. What can I do? Right now, I'm feeling fairly powerless and needing to figure out ways to be able to claim my power in a bigger way.

Sky was oscillating between staying in the USA and continuing to fight for social change, versus leaving the USA for a country that was more inclusive and accepting. Unlike the trans BIPOC who had or were considering relocating away from the USA, Sky was not concerned about how his racial identity might factor into his relocation. Relocation and considerations of place and space were not limited to emigrating from the USA, but were also relevant in considering place within the USA.

For some of the white trans participants involved with land projects (discussed in Chapter 4) or living somewhat off the

Intersectional Trans Futures

grid in rural locations, there was a simultaneous sense of fear about politics, recognition that their whiteness and social class allowed them to blend in, and a belief that their preparations for living off the grid potentially protected them from anti-trans governmental surveillance and oversight:

> We quickly learned that the folks around here just tolerate our presence, and, "You keep to your side of the fence, I'll keep to mine." There's actually a sense of reassurance in that, I feel. And my partner and I both feel like there's really no better place to be given the current political climate, because if/when things take a turn for the potential worst, we are gonna be in a spot where we're self-reliant, where we're living with people who are preppers. (Lucas, white, queer, FTM)

In part, this was in relation to concerns about being knowable to the state, when the government was potentially tracing trans people and controlling access to gender-related health care, as Amber had addressed. Living off the grid alleviated some of these concerns, but not all. However, it took a certain amount of privilege, a white settler working-class solidarity (Abelson 2019), to be more comfortable participating in these projects and spaces.

Some participants wanted to find and create new political discourses around more intersectional issues that they felt were not being addressed in the current political discourse. Switch (white, queer, nonbinary) expressed concern about intersectional issues that they felt were not being addressed, stating:

> I definitely feel sub-citizen. Oh, yeah, you get a vote, but really, where does that vote go? Is my vote really representative of my actual desires and needs? I wanna be voting on trans homelessness. I wanna be voting on how to feed single parents. There's politics that aren't addressed at the national level. I talk to my

132   Transgender Intersections

friends all the time. I said what is gonna be the single cord that strikes our country that allows us to centralize queer/ trans people of color? 'Cause I feel like that is a lens that will really start ending marginalization and oppressions, if we can centralize through that lens, 'cause these are the people who are suffering the most. That lens won't even hit – hasn't even come close to hitting our national stage. We will have national public news about white kids being shot at a high school, but we will not have national public news about every Black trans woman that has been brutally murdered, which I think is close to forty, at this moment of the year. Nobody's talking about those women. Nobody's talking about the Native women who are being trafficked . . . and are missing. These are the politics I wanna talk about, and they're not there . . . The system doesn't represent people like me. It doesn't represent the true struggles that are happening right now. My politics, as a trans person, is not there. It's not being addressed, in any kind of a way, which makes me want to move to a different country that centralizes health for trans people, or centralizes housing for trans people, or so on and so forth, has a governmental system in which it recognizes populations of people that are not being recognized as people right now in this country.

Switch referenced arguments built from bell hooks's (2000) analysis to center those who are the most marginalized in our society. If we create change to positively influence and improve the lives for those at the margins, it would also positively impact those who were already more centered. Although Switch mentions a consideration to relocate to a different country, their preference and hope was to create the change in their current community. They went on to state:

> Opening up doors for other trans people . . . I didn't realize that I was doing that. It was a weird part of my life, where I was having all of this knowledge that I was gaining, and then coming

Intersectional Trans Futures 133

into a community where I realized that that knowledge, honestly, isn't prevalent at all. That feminist critical theory is not something that people have access to. How do I bring academia back down to my [rural white working-class] community, and bring my community back up to academia, and let those two communities fully see me? It's been interesting, to say the least.

Switch hoped to serve as an agent of social change and build bridges across political divides. They particularly hoped to bring an intersectional framework to address the increasing cissexist, misogynist, ableist, settler white supremacist politics in the USA and globally.

A Call to Action

Given the systems of oppression shaping trans lives, several participants voiced their own goals or hopes for trans people to take action and create social change. Amber had recommendations for vulnerable trans people as well as those with somewhat more privilege:

I guess if you're in a position to take a little heat, I think you should be more vocal. If you are in a position where you are supremely vulnerable, I would suggest, settle down. For now just do your thing. Be quiet, find your allies, and just don't be loud.

This was her call to action to trans folks that held more privilege and were more socially and economically established. Amber hoped trans people who can will be politically active, whether that involves challenging individuals, institutions, or both.

Like Amber, Lance (Assiniboine (Nakoda) working-class trans man) also wanted to challenge some trans folks to do

134   Transgender Intersections

more when they have the privilege to do so. Lance specifically addressed white trans people's rhetorical moves that made them seem in support of trans BIPOC while taking no action to alter their own white habitus, their social circles, or their political communities. He shared:

> I see a reaction of some of the trans communities, that people are acting like we're in survival mode, even if they're white middle class and really far away from anything that could affect them . . . like you have white middle-class trans people be like "Black lives, trans Black lives matter." And I'm like, "Do you know a Black person? No? Then figure your own shit out, because that's great, but like you're not really in the reality that there's a bunch of things going on."

Lance thus named how some white trans people give lip service to whiteness, white privilege, and white supremacy, but make no real change in their own lives. His call includes white trans people moving from words to action, and moving from words to action means using an intersectional framework to change systems of power. While addressing political challenges and working towards social change were important to Lance, he was simultaneously concerned that trans people might be spending too much time on micro level issues when instead he hoped people would focus more on collective struggle:

> It's hard for us to remember what's true about us, what's right about us. It's like we may be constantly reminded about what's wrong with us. I mean, all these laws that are being written. I have a trans friend who is like, "I want to understand them all." I'm like, "You don't need to. All you need to understand is that it is oppression. That's the truth and reality of it. And we don't need to fucking dig around [or] be like 'I need to know.'" You know, it's the same pile of shit it was fifty years ago, where they're like, "you're amoral, immoral, wrong, wrong." So it's

just trying to help people see themselves in a lens where it's not about division. It's about, "How can we be together?"

His priorities for the creation of more inclusive futures involved moving beyond division towards connection.

Lance's question, "How can we be together?," was addressed by a number of participants. They resoundingly talked about relationships and bridge building as keys to creating better trans futures. Some of the biggest themes discussed by trans BIPOC were in relation to the ways social media and the media more broadly continually reinforced divisions, created barriers to solidarity across difference, and increased infighting within communities. As Joe (Black, nonbinary, pansexual) shared: "We have to start coming together. I don't have to agree with everything. We don't even have to be two people that are talking. But as a people, we need to come together and fight together." As Joe notes, community and coalition building are important in creating a sense of belongingness and a sense of visibility. Valentina (twenty-year-old white queer transgender woman) similarly addressed the importance of trans people, and more broadly, those that are 2SLGBTQIA+, forming community:

> It would be nice if the community was a little more community, rather than being so isolated and apart in the different communes. If there was some sort of event or venue where we could all come together and make it clear, like, "We are a valuable demographic in the area worthwhile of attention and service," that would be helpful. Just to see, "Yes, we exist. We are here." A lot of people are unaware of that just due to the communal nature and want of isolation in the [rural] area.

Valentina was talking about how multiple 2SLGBTQIA+ communities existed in her region but operated in their own spheres of influence. Some of these communities, in part due to settler whiteness, were able to blend in with the more

136 Transgender Intersections

conservative areas, as noted in Chapter 4. Valentina hoped a more unified community might be built from those and offer greater support, particularly to younger trans people.

Lance also desired building community across difference, and he noted that community building requires reflection on positionality in relation to systems of power:

> Some of the nonbinary people are like, "I'm not even in your system, so I'm out. I'm not even gonna, like, why would I even be involved in that?" It's usually white people, but that's difficult to hear, you know? Because it's like you're taking yourself out of this equation.

Lance strongly believed that an individual had to hold a certain amount of privilege to consider themselves "outside the system" if that meant not needing to be involved in changing the system, and that this was particularly true for white people. For Lance, and many of our other participants, considering oneself outside the system meant you still benefit from a system that is oppressive. Like Amber, who mentioned "If you're in a position to take a little heat, I think you should be more vocal," Lance and others encouraged those with more institutional and structural power – in this case, white nonbinary people – to move forward and help create inclusive communities.

Elle (Chinese American queer trans woman) also addressed the importance of community through collectively strategizing and shifting the cultural narrative:

> We haven't been strategizing collectively on what brings us together on a common ground . . . I don't think we collectively have done enough to make [trans issues] relatable or contributive to society. And I'm just saying that, as someone who's now stepped outside of the USA . . . it's interesting. I was just chatting to our head of comms last night at my company. She's like, "yeah, we're not targeting the center enough. We're trying to

Intersectional Trans Futures 137

always get the extreme opposite end." But they're never going to change. And turning to our own constituents? Well, they already bought it. That doesn't help. How to expand the base, right? And that's not easy, because I think there is so much we need as a community on an individual and collective basis, which puts us at a disadvantage.

Elle was not disheartened by these challenges but was instead thinking strategically about how to come together across different needs. This discord within trans communities was of concern to a number of participants; as Dante stated, "if we turn into the things that we're fighting, then we've lost the entire war."

Jacobo (Chicano heterosexual trans man) reflected on the ways increased visibility and community building might have ripple effects in our broader society. Similar to many of our other trans BIPOC, this came down to relationships and the importance of connecting across differences. He shared:

So I think it starts on a smaller level here within your own community, within your own life and the people, you know? And I think it has a ripple effect. It's like you throw a rock into a lake and that ripple effect eventually starts getting bigger. So I hope that things change in the future. I think that there is a lot of positivity now. And you know, between TV shows and movies and actors coming out [as trans], more books being written and presentations being done on trans people, and I think the visibility is bigger now than it was back then [sixteen years ago], which is good. And I think people just have to keep fighting for that. And I think here in this mix of the USA, that we have . . . some places where it's safe and some places when it's not. People are leaving in droves from Florida and from other places where it's not safe to be trans and be LGBT, and so it'll be interesting to see how that changes and how this affects stuff.

138   Transgender Intersections

Jacobo spoke specifically about how he engaged in the work to create these ripple effects in his own life and communities. For him, it meant recognizing his own privilege, actively engaging in work towards change, supporting diverse organizations, and reaching out to individuals across differences. It also meant finding communities that supported him and the future he was working towards.

*   *   *

To create the change many participants wanted – a more trans-inclusive future – means acknowledging privileges, fostering understanding through differences, and building coalitions, all while centering those whose experiences are more socially marginalized. The work of world building requires orienting towards intersectionality, and that means building community through and across differences. We return one final time to Lance, who reminds us: "We need to keep inviting people back into the equation. Struggle with us. Have fun with us."

Sometimes this work for intersectional social change can feel overwhelming and frustrating. We may experience only the struggle. Yet, what if, through intersectional community, we could experience more of the empowerment and pleasure of finding connection in both similarity and difference and of creating the ripples of social change? What if we approach this as both work for a better world as well as joy in the process? Lance and many of our other participants invite us to do just that: to imagine the intersectional futures we want for ourselves and each other, and to begin to work on them individually, interpersonally, and structurally.

Appendix: Methodology

Data and Analysis

The analysis in this book draws from four research projects. The first data set is from an ethnography consisting of interviews and participant observation with trans BIPOC in the southern, midwestern, southwestern, and western regions of the USA between 2005 and 2009. This data was collected by Kylan Mattias de Vries, and as with all the data sets, participants chose their names for the research. It includes qualitative, in-depth, semi-structured interviews and focus groups with twenty-nine trans BIPOC, as well as over 100 hours of participant observation at four national transgender conferences, planning committees for Black trans conferences, and several online groups for trans people of color. Interviews were also conducted with two white trans people. Interviews were conducted in person at a location chosen by the participant (such as their home or a local restaurant) and lasted one to three-and-a-half hours. Using a conversational approach, open and closed questions, and "interviewing by comment" (Snow, Zurcher and Sjoberg 1982), participants were asked about five broad areas: self-identification; interactions with

140   Appendix

family and friends; perceptions, experiences, and presentation of self in relation to interactions with "others" (i.e., acquaintances, co-workers, strangers); perceptions, experiences, and presentation of self in relation to specific communities (e.g., transgender, racial, cultural, religious, academic); and perceptions, experiences, and presentation of self in relation to the medical community. Research participants were recruited through a number of transgender social networks using snowball sampling. This research was approved by the Southern Illinois University Institutional Review Board.

A second data set includes thirty-five in-depth, semi-structured, qualitative interviews conducted with the partners of trans people, including trans partners of trans people, between 2013 and 2015. Data for this set was collected by Carey Jean Sojka. Participants were living in the USA at the time, were currently in a relationship with someone who was trans, and had been in that relationship through one or more types of transition-related change such as social transition experiences and/or medically assisted transition processes. The call for participants expressed particular interest in interviewing people of color, people in interracial relationships, men or masculine-identified people, and/or trans people as part of purposive snowball sampling. Interviews were conducted primarily via video conferencing or phone, with a few interviews conducted in person at gatherings or conferences. The interview guide included questions about their identities and experiences, particularly in relation to gender, race, and sexuality; their experiences during their relationship and their experiences in relation to their partners' transition; bodies and embodiment; community; demographics; and social change. Follow-up and probe questions were also included throughout interviews. Interviews lasted between forty-eight minutes and three hours and forty-eight minutes, depending on the responses and interest of the participant. For the purposes of this book, the data from this second data set was included only to support themes

Appendix

that were already identified in relation to the first, third, and fourth data sets. This research was approved by the University at Albany, SUNY, Institutional Review Board.

A third data set is an ethnography with data collected from 2017 to 2019 involving interviews and participant observation focused on racialization and, particularly, whiteness among predominantly white rural trans and/or nonbinary people but also including BIPOC rural trans and/or nonbinary people. Data was collected by both authors. This ethnography was situated in the region of Northern California and Southern Oregon, which both share some aspects of a regional identity, including a conservative, white normative, and heteronormative libertarian rural ethos in a liberal-leaning state. Participant observation included fifty-five hours of in-person trans community peer group participation and over 100 hours observing online regionally focused trans peer support groups. In addition, twenty-seven adult trans people (ages twenty-four to eighty-two), seventeen trans youth (ages nineteen to twenty-three; we did not conduct interviews with minors), ten partners of trans people, and five parents of trans children were interviewed. Prior to the interview, participants completed a short demographic survey. Participants then chose the location for their interview; the majority were conducted in person at a location of the participants' choice, such as a library or coffee shop, and a few participants chose video conferencing or telephone interviews. Using open-ended questions, interviews began with respondents sharing about their gender experiences, particularly in relation to their rural environment. The demographic survey was then used for more focused questions in relation to participants' identities (such as racial identities), connections with communities, interactions with others, and experiences with various institutions (family, education, health care, law/criminal justice system, social services, and politics). The final questions centered on social change. Research participants were recruited through a number of transgender

142   Appendix

social networks using snowball sampling. This research was approved by the Southern Oregon University Institutional Review Board.

A fourth data set includes longitudinal interviews conducted with research participants from the first data set. Of the twenty-nine original trans BIPOC participants, about half had shared contact information during the original data collection with a request to stay in touch, and they were recontacted to ask if they would like to participate in a follow-up interview. Of that half who were recontacted, eight individuals agreed to be interviewed; for the others, some contact information was no longer in use by the participant (e.g., indicated by failed email deliveries), one participant was interested but was unable to find time for the interview during the research period, and we were also aware that two participants (perhaps more) had since died. The research was conducted by both Carey Jean Sojka and Kylan Mattias de Vries, and interviews were conducted via video conferencing by Kylan Mattias de Vries with the eight trans BIPOC participants in 2023. The same pseudonyms were used, and the data from these interviews was also used as a longitudinal comparison to the early study data. The interviews began with sharing participants' identity-related answers from the original interview along with questions about how they identified now. Similar to the first interviews, questions centered on interactions with others and institutions. We added two questions: one about the current political climate, and one about imagining a future where they, and those who share their identities, would thrive. This research was approved by the Southern Oregon University Institutional Review Board.

Overall, the majority of the book has utilized data from the first and fourth data sets; data from one or both of these sets is included and analyzed in every chapter. Data from the second data set has only been used minimally, when discussing the experiences of some partners of transgender people, and data from the third data set was mostly analyzed only in the fourth,

Appendix 143

fifth, and sixth chapters. While the vast majority of research participants included in this book are trans, we interviewed some family members of trans people, as detailed above. While a much smaller subset in this book, they provided another frame of interactions that they witnessed their trans partner or trans child experiencing. Some of them were also themselves trans, and in those cases they shared some comparisons of their own experiences with what they observed in their partner or child.

Interviews from all data sets were transcribed verbatim. Data from each of these sets was analyzed using grounded theory methods (Strauss and Corbin 1990). We used open coding, identifying common themes and issues, as well as what Emerson, Fretz, and Shaw (1995) refer to as focused coding, creating categories and examining the connections between them. As we reengaged in data analysis for this book, we communicated with each other about our processes in terms of analyzing and theorizing (Strauss and Corbin 1990). Data analysis for the third and fourth data sets was collaboratively completed by both authors.

This data spans almost twenty years, and thus some social contexts have shifted. Data analysis for the first, second, and third data sets was initially done independently for each set around the time the data was collected, while our analysis then brought all four data sets together as they are in this book. Both the older and the more recent data tell us about social processes of identification, interaction, negotiations, and broader connections to systems of power.

Positionality

As this book addresses, the intersections of social identities matter greatly to our experiences and our relationships to power. As researchers, our positionality influences our

144   Appendix

analytical lens, as well as determining what social phenomena we deem to be important. Our work recognizes the importance of standpoint theory (Collins 1986; Smith 1990) in intersectionality theory, and as such, we want to call attention to the ways that our various identities influence this book.

For instance, as two white researchers, our whiteness shapes our approach to intersectional analysis. We recognize that we do not have lived experience of being marginalized or oppressed because of our race in a white supremacist society. We are both settlers, and recognize that we do not have lived experience as Native or Indigenous people in a settler colonial society. We approach this work with humility, doing our best to stay true to the voices of our BIPOC research participants who do have that lived experience, and recognizing that we may have made mistakes. We also know that even in ways we hold marginalized identities (as trans or nonbinary, as disabled, and others), our experiences do not make us experts on the experiences of others with those shared identities, in part because of differences across intersectional categories and also because each category is diverse and expansive.

In our research, we each, in different projects, disclosed aspects of our identities through the research process. For instance, de Vries shared identities as a "white, queer, working-class [at the time], trans guy raised in Canada" during his first data collection. Many participants discussed "bad experiences" with other research projects (Weston 2004), and de Vries's insider status as trans addressed some concerns. De Vries also highlighted having Canadian bicultural (Dutch/Canadian) identity and minimal experiential knowledge of race relations across the USA (for an interrogation of this process, see de Vries 2015). Sojka shared identity aspects during data collection for the second and third data sets, including being the partner of a trans person when interviewing partners of trans people, as well as discussing other identities, including whiteness, with participants in back and forth discussions.

Appendix

Our relationship to our research also includes our relationship to the scholars and activists who have made this work possible. As Ahmed shares: "Citation is feminist memory. Citation is how we acknowledge our debt to those who came before; those who helped us find our way when the way was obscured because we deviated from the paths we were told to follow" (2017:15–16). We want to acknowledge the tremendous debt we have to those who came before us, who have done and continue to do the scholarly and activist work to build an intersectional framework which both describes our world and contributes to building a better, more just world. We particularly recognize that the work of women of color is foundational to intersectionality, and we are indebted to those scholars and activists who have led the way and who continue to be leaders in this work.

References

Abelson, Miriam J. 2014. "Dangerous Privilege: Trans Men, Masculinities, and Changing Perceptions of Safety." *Sociological Forum* 29(3):549–70.

Abelson, Miriam J. 2016a. "'You Aren't from Around Here': Race, Masculinity, and Rural Transgender Men." *Gender, Place & Culture* 23(11):1535–46.

Abelson, Miriam J. 2016b. "Trans Men Engaging, Reforming, and Resisting Feminisms." *TSQ: Transgender Studies Quarterly* 3(1–2):15–21.

Abelson, Miriam J. 2019. *Men in Place: Trans Masculinity, Race, and Sexuality in America*. Minneapolis: University of Minnesota Press.

Ahmed, Sara. 2007. "A Phenomenology of Whiteness." *Feminist Theory* 8(2):149–68.

Ahmed, Sara. 2017. *Living a Feminist Life*. Durham, NC: Duke University Press.

Aizura, Aren Z. 2006. "Of Borders and Homes: The Imaginary Community of (Trans)Sexual Citizenship." *Inter-Asia Cultural Studies* 7(2):289–309.

Aizura, Aren Z. 2010. "Feminine Transformations: Gender Reassignment Surgical Tourism in Thailand." *Medical Anthropology* 29(4):424–43.

References

Alimahomed, Sabrina. 2010. "Thinking Outside the Rainbow: Women of Color Redefining Queer Politics and Identity." *Social Identities* 16(2):151–68.

Altheide, David L. 2000. "Identity and the Definition of the Situation in a Mass-Mediated Context." *Symbolic Interaction* 23(1):1–27.

Anthias, Floya. 2013. "Intersectionality What? Social Divisions, Intersectionality and Levels of Analysis." *Ethnicities* 13(1):3–19.

Anzaldúa, Gloria. 2007. *Borderlands/La Frontera: The New Mestiza.* 3rd edition. Aunt Lute Books.

Atwood, S., Thekla Morgenroth, and Kristina R. Olson. 2024. "Gender Essentialism and Benevolent Sexism in Anti-Trans Rhetoric." *Social Issues and Policy Review* 18(1):171–93.

Azhar, Sameena, Antonia R. G. Alvarez, Anne S. J. Farina, and Susan Klumpner. 2021. "'You're So Exotic Looking': An Intersectional Analysis of Asian American and Pacific Islander Stereotypes." *Affilia* 36(3):282–301.

Beauchamp, Toby Cason. 2010. *Going Stealth: Transgender Bodies and U.S. Surveillance Practices.* Durham, NC: Duke University Press.

Betancourt, Roland. 2020. *Byzantine Intersectionality: Sexuality, Gender, and Race in the Middle Ages.* Princeton, NJ: Princeton University Press.

Bey, Marquis. 2017. "The Trans*-ness of Blackness, The Blackness of Trans*-ness." *Transgender Studies Quarterly* 4(2):275–95.

Bey, Marquis. 2022. *Black Trans Feminism.* Durham, NC: Duke University Press.

binaohan, b. 2014. *decolonizing trans/gender 101.* Toronto, Canada: biyuti publishing.

Blumer, Herbert. 1969. *Symbolic Interactionism: Perspective and Method.* Englewood Cliffs, NJ: Prentice-Hall.

Bockting, Walter, Renato Barucco, Allen LeBlanc, Anneliese Singh, William Mellman, Curtis Dolezal, and Anke Ehrhardt. 2020. "Sociopolitical Change and Transgender People's Perceptions of Vulnerability and Resilience." *Sexuality Research and Social Policy* 17:162–74.

148 References

Boellstorff, Tom, Mauro Cabral, Micha Cárdenas, Trystan Cotten, Eric A. Stanley, Kalanopua Young, and Aren Z. Aizura. 2014. "Decolonizing Transgender: A Round Table Discussion." *Transgender Studies Quarterly* 1(3):419–39.

Bohrer, Ashley J. 2019. *Marxism and Intersectionality: Race, Gender, Class and Sexuality under Contemporary Capitalism.* Bielefeld: transcript Verlag.

Bonilla-Silva, Eduardo. 1996. "Rethinking Racism: Toward a Structural Interpretation." *American Sociological Review* 62(3):465–80.

Bonilla-Silva, Eduardo. 2003. *Racism without Racists: Color-blind Racism and the Persistence of Racial Inequality in the United States.* Lanham, MD: Rowman and Littlefield.

Boutyline, Andrei, and Laura K. Soter. 2021. "Cultural Schemas: What They Are, How to Find Them, and What to Do Once You've Caught One." *American Sociological Review* 86(4):728–58.

Brekhus, Wayne. 1998. "A Sociology of the Unmarked: Redirecting Our Focus." *Sociological Theory* 16(1):34–51.

Brooms, Derrick R., and Jelisa S. Clark. 2020. "Black Misandry and the Killing of Black Boys and Men." *Sociological Focus* 53(2):125–40.

Brubaker, Rogers. 2018. *Trans: Gender and Race in an Age of Unsettled Identities.* Princeton, NJ: Princeton University Press.

Brumbaugh-Johnson, Stacey M., and Kathleen E. Hull. 2019. "Coming Out as Transgender: Navigating the Social Implications of a Transgender Identity." *Journal of Homosexuality* 66(8):1148–77.

Burton, Linda M., Eduardo Bonilla-Silva, Victor Ray, Rose Buckelew, and Elizabeth Hordge Freeman. 2010. "Critical Race Theories, Colorism, and the Decade's Research on Families of Color." *Journal of Marriage and Family* 72(3):440–59.

Cerezo, Alison, Mariah Cummings, Meredith Holmes, and Chelsey Williams. 2020. "Identity as Resistance: Identity Formation at the Intersection of Race, Gender Identity, and Sexual Orientation." *Psychology of Women Quarterly* 44(1):67–83.

Chan, Christian D. 2018. "Families as Transformative Allies to Trans Youth of Color: Positioning Intersectionality as Analysis to

References

Demarginalize Political Systems of Oppression." *Journal of GLBT Family Studies* 14(1–2):43–60.

Charlebois, Justin. 2012. "The Discursive Construction of 'Bounded Masculinity/Unbounded Femininity.'" *Journal of Gender Studies* 21(2):201–14.

Charmaz, Kathy, Scott R. Harris, and Leslie Irvine. 2019. *The Social Self and Everyday Life: Understanding the World through Symbolic Interactionism.* Hoboken, NJ: John Wiley & Sons.

Chaudhry, V. Varun. 2019. "Trans/Coalitional Love-Politics: Black Feminisms and the Radical Possibilities of Transgender Studies." *Transgender Studies Quarterly* 6(4):521–38.

Chavez-Dueñas, Nayeli Y., Hector Y. Adames, Jessica G. Perez-Chavez, and Silvia P. Salas. 2019. "Healing Ethno-Racial Trauma in Latinx Immigrant Communities: Cultivating Hope, Resistance, and Action." *The American Psychologist* 74(1):49–62.

Chen, Jian Neo. 2019. *Trans Exploits: Trans of Color Cultures and Technologies in Movement.* Durham, NC: Duke University Press.

Chong, Kelly H., and Nadia Y. Kim. 2022. "'The Model Man': Shifting Perceptions of Asian American Masculinity and the Renegotiation of a Racial Hierarchy of Desire." *Men and Masculinities* 25(5):674–97.

Chou, Rosalind S., and Joe R. Feagin. 2008. *The Myth of the Model Minority: Asian Americans Facing Racism.* Boulder, CO: Paradigm Publishers.

Chudyk, Elliot. 2023. "Genderplay: Reclaiming and Reconfiguring Femininity through the Gendered Labor Practices of Transmasculine Sex Workers." *Social Problems*, https://doi.org /10.1093/socpro/spad043.

Clare, Eli. 1999. *Exile and Pride: Disability, Queerness, and Liberation.* Cambridge, MA: South End Press.

Collins, Patricia Hill. 1986. "Learning from the Outsider Within: The Sociological Significance of Black Feminist Thought." *Social Problems* 33(6):514–32.

References

Collins, Patricia Hill. 1993. "Toward a New Vision: Race, Class, and Gender as Categories of Analysis and Connection." *Race, Sex & Class* 1(1):25–45.

Collins, Patricia Hill. 2000. *Black Feminist Thought: Knowledge, Consciousness, and the Politics of Empowerment.* 2nd ed. New York: Routledge.

Collins, Patricia Hill. 2005. *Black Sexual Politics: African Americans, Gender, and the New Racism.* New York: Routledge.

Collins, Patricia Hill, and Sirma Bilge. 2020. *Intersectionality.* 2nd ed. Cambridge: Polity Press.

Collins, Patricia Hill, Lionel A. Maldonado, Dana Y. Takagi, Barrie Thorne, Lynn Weber, and Howard Winant. 1995. "Symposium: On West and Fenstermaker's 'Doing Difference.'" *Gender & Society* 9(4):491–513.

Combahee River Collective. 1995. "A Black Feminist Statement." In *Words of Fire: An Anthology of African-American Feminist Thought,* edited by B. Guy-Sheftall. New York: The New Press, pp. 232–40.

Connell, Raewyn. 1987. *Gender and Power: Society, the Person, and Sexual Politics.* Cambridge: Polity Press.

Connell, Raewyn. 2005. *Masculinities.* Cambridge: Polity Press.

Connell, Raewyn. 2009. "Accountable Conduct: 'Doing Gender' in Transsexual and Political Retrospect." *Gender & Society* 23(1):104–11.

Connell, Raewyn, and James W. Messerschmidt. 2005. "Hegemonic Masculinity: Rethinking the Concept." *Gender & Society* 19(6):829–59.

Cooley, Charles Horton. [1902] 1964. *Human Nature and the Social Order.* New York: Schocken.

Corbin, Juliet M., and Anselm Strauss. 1990. "Grounded Theory Research: Procedures, Canons, and Evaluative Criteria." *Qualitative Sociology* 13(1):3–21.

Crenshaw, Kimberlé. 1989. "Demarginalizing the Intersection of Race and Sex: A Black Feminist Critique of Antidiscrimination

References

151

Doctrine, Feminist Theory and Antiracist Politics." *University of Chicago Legal Forum* 140:139–67.

Crenshaw, Kimberlé. 1991. "Mapping the Margins: Identity Politics, Intersectionality, and Violence Against Women." *Stanford Law Review* 43(6):1241–99.

Cromwell, Jason. 1999. *Transmen and FTMs: Identities, Bodies, Genders, and Sexualities.* Urbana: University of Illinois Press.

Curington, Celeste Vaughan. 2016. "Rethinking Multiracial Formation in the United States: Toward an Intersectional Approach." *Sociology of Race and Ethnicity* 2(1):27–41.

Daniel, G. Reginald, Laura Kina, Wei Ming Dariotis, and Camilla Fojas. 2014. "Emerging Paradigms in Critical Mixed Race Studies." *Journal of Critical Mixed Race Studies* 1(1):6–65.

Davis, Kathy. 2008. "Intersectionality as Buzzword: A Sociology of Science Perspective on What Makes a Feminist Theory Successful." *Feminist Theory* 9(1):67–85.

Davis, Stephanie. 2023. *Queer and Trans People of Colour in the UK.* New York: Routledge.

de Vries, Kylan Mattias. 2012. "Intersectional Identities and Conceptions of the Self: The Experience of Transgender People." *Symbolic Interaction* 35(1):49–67.

de Vries, Kylan Mattias. 2015. "Transgender People of Color at the Center: Conceptualizing a New Intersectional Model." *Ethnicities* 15(1):3–27.

Dozier, Raine. 2005. "Beards, Breasts, and Bodies: Doing Sex in a Gendered World." *Gender & Society* 19(3):297–317.

Draut, Tamara. 2018. *Sleeping Giant: The Untapped Economic and Political Power of America's New Working Class.* New York: Anchor.

Emerson, Robert M., Rachel L. Fretz, and Linda L. Shaw. 1995. *Writing Ethnographic Fieldnotes.* Chicago, IL: University of Chicago Press.

Erdmans, Mary Patrice. 2004. "Looking for Angel: White Working-Class Women Lost between Identities." *Race, Gender & Class* 11(4):48–62.

References

Erel, Umut, Jin Haritaworn, Encarnación Gutiérrez Rodríguez, and Christian Klesse. 2008. "On the Depoliticisation of Intersectionality Talk: Conceptualising Multiple Oppressions in Critical Sexuality Studies." In *Out of Place: Interrogating Silences in Queerness/ Raciality*, edited by A. Kuntsman and M. Esperanza. New York: Raw Nerve Books, pp. 265–92.

Espiritu, Yen Le. 1992. *Asian American Panethnicity: Bridging Institutions and Identities.* Philadelphia, PA: Temple University Press.

Feagin, Joe R., and José A. Corbes. 2008. "Latinos/as and White Racial Frame: The Procrustean Bed of Assimilation." *Sociological Inquiry* 78(1):39–53.

Ferguson, Roderick A. 2018. *One-Dimensional Queer.* Cambridge: Polity Press.

Fischer, Mia. 2019. *Terrorizing Gender: Transgender Visibility and the Surveillance Practices of the U.S. Security State.* Lincoln: University of Nebraska Press.

Franks, Myfanwy. 2000. "Crossing the Borders of Whiteness? White Muslim Women Who Wear the Hijab in Britain Today." *Ethnic and Racial Studies* 23(5):917–29.

Friedman, Susan Stanford. 2015. "Religion, Intersectionality, and Queer/Feminist Narrative Theory: The Bildungsromane of Ahdaf Soueif, Leila Aboulela, and Randa Jarrar." In *Narrative Theory Unbound: Queer and Feminist Interventions*, edited by R. Warhol and S. S. Lanser. Columbus: Ohio State University Press, pp. 101–22.

Galarte, Francisco J. 2021. *Brown Trans Figurations: Rethinking Race, Gender, and Sexuality in Chicanx/Latinx Studies.* Austin: University of Texas Press.

Gamson, Joshua, and Dawne Moon. 2004. "The Sociology of Sexualities: Queer and Beyond." *Annual Review of Sociology* 30:47–64.

Garrett, Rhianna. 2024. "'I'm Not White': Counter-Stories from 'Mixed Race' Women Navigating PhDs." *Equality, Diversity and Inclusion: An International Journal*, https://doi.org/10.1108/EDI -03-2023-0097.

Gill-Peterson, Jules. 2018. *Histories of the Transgender Child.* Minneapolis: University of Minnesota Press.

References

Glenn, Evelyn Nakano. 2002. *Unequal Freedom: How Race and Gender Shaped American Citizenship and Labor*. Cambridge, MA: Harvard University Press.

Goffman, Erving. 1959. *The Presentation of Self in Everyday Life*. New York: Doubleday.

Goffman, Erving. 1963. *Stigma: Notes on the Management of a Spoiled Identity*. London: Pelican Books.

Goffman, Erving. 1974. *Frame Analysis: An Essay on the Organization of Experience*. London: Harper and Row.

Goldsen, Karen I. Fredriksen, Meghan Romanelli, Charles P. Hoy-Ellis, and Hailey Jung. 2022. "Health, Economic and Social Disparities Among Transgender Women, Transgender Men and Transgender Nonbinary Adults: Results from a Population-Based Study." *Preventive Medicine* 156:106988.

Gonzales, Gabrielle G. 2019. "Embodied Resistance: Multiracial Identity, Gender, and the Body." *Social Sciences* 8(8):1–16.

Gossett, Reina, Eric A. Stanley, and Johanna Burton, eds. 2017. *Trap Door: Trans Cultural Production and the Politics of Visibility*. Cambridge, MA: MIT Press.

Goulding, Cathlin. 2019. "Walking the Places of Exception: The Tule Lake National Monument." *Journal of Public Pedagogies* 4:52–8.

Grabham, Emily. 2009. "Intersectionality: Traumatic Impressions." In *Intersectionality and Beyond*, edited by E. Grabham, E. Cooper, J. Krishnadas, and D. Herman. New York: Routledge-Cavendish, pp. 183–201.

Green, Kai M., and Marquis Bey. 2017. "Where Black Feminist Thought and Trans* Feminism Meet: A Conversation." *Souls* 19(4):438–54.

Gundemeda, Nagaraju. 2020. "Caste in Twenty First Century India: Sociological Reflections on University Students' Perceptions in South India." *Asian & African Studies* 29(1):89–110.

Halberstam, Jack, and C. Jacob Hale. 1998. "Butch/FTM Border Wars: A Note on Collaboration." *GLQ: A Journal of Lesbian and Gay Studies* 4(2):283–5.

Hamer, Katarzyna, Sam McFarland, Barbara Czarnecka, Agnieszka

References

Golińska, Liliana Manrique Cadena, Magdalena Łużniak-Piecha, and Tomasz Jułkowski. 2020. "What is an 'Ethnic Group' in Ordinary People's Eyes? Different Ways of Understanding It Among American, British, Mexican, and Polish Respondents." *Cross-Cultural Research* 54(1):28–72.

Han, Chong-suk. 2009. "Asian Girls are Prettier: Gendered Presentations as Stigma Management Among Gay Asian Men." *Symbolic Interaction* 22(2):106–22.

Haraway, Donna. 1988. "Situated Knowledges: The Science Question in Feminism and the Privilege of Partial Perspective." *Feminist Studies* 14(3):575–99.

Haritaworn, Jin. 2008. "Shifting Positionalities: Empirical Reflections on a Queer/Trans of Colour Methodology." *Sociological Research Online* 13(1):162–73.

Haritaworn, Jin. 2009. "Hybrid Border-Crossers? Towards a Radical Socialisation of 'Mixed-Race.'" *Journal of Ethnic and Migration Studies* 35(1):115–32.

Haritaworn, Jin. 2010. "Queer Injuries: The Racial Politics of 'Homophobic Hate Crime' in Germany." *Social Justice* 37(1):69–85.

Heidenreich, Linda. 2020. *Nepantla Squared: Transgender Mestiz@ Histories in Times of Global Shift*. Lincoln: University of Nebraska Press.

Holla, Sylvia, and Giselinde Kuipers. 2016. "Aesthetic Capital." In *Routledge International Handbook for the Sociology of Art and Culture*, edited by L. Hanquinet and M. Savage. London: Routledge, pp. 290–304.

Holm, Tom, J., Diane Pearson, and Ben Chavis. 2003. "Peoplehood: A Model for the Extension of Sovereignty in American Indian Studies." *Wicazo Sa Review* 18(1):7–24.

hooks, bell. 2000. *Feminist Theory: From Margin to Center*. 2nd ed. Boston, MA: South End.

Horowitz, David A. 1989. "The Klansman as Outsider: Ethnocultural Solidarity and Antielitism in the Oregon Ku Klux Klan of the 1920s." *The Pacific Northwest Quarterly* 80(1):12–20.

References

Hoston, William T. 2018. *Toxic Silence: Race, Black Gender Identity, and Addressing the Violence Against Black Transgender Women in Houston.* New York: Peter Lang.

Howard, Judith A., and Daniel G. Renfrow. 2014. "Intersectionality." In *Handbook of the Social Psychology of Inequality*, edited by J. D. McLeod, E. J. Lawler, and M. Schwalbe. New York: Springer, pp. 95–124.

Howard, Susanna D., Kevin L. Lee, Aviva G. Nathan, Hannah C. Wenger, Marshall H. Chin, and Scott C. Cook. 2019. "Healthcare Experiences of Transgender People of Color." *Journal of General Internal Medicine* 34(10):2068–74.

Hsu, V. Jo. 2022. *Constellating Home: Trans and Queer Asian American Rhetorics.* Columbus: Ohio State University Press.

Ifekwunigwe, Jayne O., ed. 2004. *"Mixed Race" Studies: A Reader.* New York: Routledge.

Ineese-Nash, Nicole. 2020. "Is Resistance Enough? Reflections of Identity, Politics, and Relations in the 'In-Between' Spaces of Indigeneity and Settlerhood." *AlterNative: An International Journal of Indigenous Peoples* 16(1):10–17.

James, Sandy E., Jody L. Herman, Laura E. Durso, and Rodrigo Heng-Lehtinen. 2024. *Early Insights: A Report of the 2022 U.S. Transgender Survey.* Washington, DC: National Center for Transgender Equality.

James, Sandy E., Jody L. Herman, Susan Rankin, Mara Keisling, Lisa Mottet, and Ma'ayan Anafi. 2016. *The Report of the 2015 U.S. Transgender Survey.* Washington, DC: National Center for Transgender Equality.

Jesperson, Jamey. 2022. "Settler *Trans*Nationalism: The Colonial Politics of White Trans Passing on Stolen Land." *Spectator* 42(1):32–43.

Johanssen, Jacob. 2021. *Fantasy, Online Misogyny and the Manosphere: Male Bodies of Dis/inhibition.* New York: Routledge.

Josephson, Tristan. 2023. *On Transits and Transitions: Trans Migrants and U.S. Immigration Law.* New Brunswick, NJ: Rutgers University Press.

156 References

Joshi, Khyati Y. 2021. *White Christian Privilege: The Illusion of Religious Equality in America*. New York: NYU Press.

Kafer, Alison. 2013. *Feminist, Queer, Crip*. Bloomington: Indiana University Press.

Keith, Katie. 2022. "HHS Issues Guidance to Help Protect Transgender Youth." *Health Affairs Forefront*, www.healthaffairs.org.

Khanna, Nikki. 2004. "The Role of Reflected Appraisals in Racial Identity: The Case of Multiracial Asians." *Social Psychology Quarterly* 67(2):115–31.

Koyama, Emi. 2006. "Whose Feminism is It Anyway? The Unspoken Racism of the Trans Inclusion Debate." In *The Transgender Studies Reader*, edited by S. Stryker and S. Whittle. New York: Routledge, pp. 698–705.

Krell, Elías Cosenza. 2017. "Is Transmisogyny Killing Trans Women of Color? Black Trans Feminisms and the Exigencies of White Femininity." *TSQ: Transgender Studies Quarterly* 4(2):226–42.

Kuper, Laura E., M. Brett Cooper, and Megan A. Mooney. 2022. "Supporting and Advocating for Transgender and Gender Diverse Youth and Their Families Within the Sociopolitical Context of Widespread Discriminatory Legislation and Policies." *Clinical Practice in Pediatric Psychology* 10(3):336–45.

Laing, Marie. 2021. *Urban Indigenous Youth Reframing Two-Spirit*. New York: Routledge.

Laing, Tony. 2017. "Black Masculinities Expressed Through, and Constrained by, Brotherhood." *The Journal of Men's Studies* 25(2):168–97.

Lamble, Sarah. 2008. "Retelling Racialized Violence, Remaking White Innocence: The Politics of Interlocking Oppressions in Transgender Day of Remembrance." *Sexuality Research & Social Policy* 5(1):24–42.

Laumann, Edward O., John H. Gagnon, Robert T. Michael, and Stuart Michaels. 1994. *The Social Organization of Sexuality: Sexual Practices in the United States*. Chicago, IL: University of Chicago Press.

Lewis, Amanda E. 2004. "'What Group?' Studying Whites and

References

Whiteness in the Era of 'Color-Blindness.'" *Sociological Theory* 22(4):623–46.

Lie, Nadia. 2014. "From Latin to Latino Lover: Hispanicity and Female Desire in Popular Culture." *Journal of Popular Romance Studies* 4(1):1–18.

Lipsitz, George. 2006. *The Possessive Investment in Whiteness: How White People Profit from Identity Politics.* Philadelphia, PA: Temple University Press.

Loewen, James. 2005. *Sundown Towns: A Hidden Dimension of American Racism.* New York: The New Press.

Lofland, John, David Snow, Leon Anderson, and Lyn H. Lofland. 2006. *Analyzing Social Settings: A Guide to Qualitative Observation and Analysis.* 4th ed. Belmont, CA: Wadsworth/Thomson Learning.

Ludvig, Alice. 2006. "Differences Between Women? Intersecting Voices in a Female Narrative." *European Journal of Women's Studies* 13(3):245–58.

Luibheid, Eithne, and Karma R. Chávez, eds. 2020. *Queer and Trans Migrations: Dynamics of Illegalization, Detention, and Deportation.* Urbana: University of Illinois Press.

Lutz, Helma. 2002. "The Long Shadows of the Past. The New Europe at a Crossroad." In *Crossing Borders and Shifting Boundaries, Vol. II: Gender, Identities, and Networks*, edited by I. Lenz, H. Lutz, M. Morokvasic-Müller, C. Schöning-Kalender, and H. Schwenken. Opladen: Leske and Budrich, pp. 57–73.

Lutz, Helma, Maria Teresa Herrara Vivar, and Linda Supik, eds. 2011. *Framing Intersectionality: Debates on a Multi-Faceted Concept in Gender Studies.* Farnham: Ashgate Publishing.

McCall, George J., and Jerry Laird Simmons. 1966. *Identities and Interactions.* New York: Free Press.

McCall, Leslie. 2005. "The Complexity of Intersectionality." *Signs* 30(3):1771–800.

McKay, Dwanna L. 2021. "Real Indians: Policing or Protecting Authentic Indigenous Identity?" *Sociology of Race and Ethnicity* 7(1):12–25.

References

Madley, Benjamin. 2016. *An American Genocide: The United States and the California Indian Catastrophe, 1846–1873*. New Haven, CT: Yale University Press.

Majors, Richard, and Janet Mancini Billson. 1992. *Cool Pose: The Dilemmas of Black Manhood in America*. New York: Touchstone.

Manalansan, Martin F. 2015. "Bakla (Philippines)." In *International Encyclopedia of Human Sexuality*, edited by P. Whelehan and A. Bolin. Hoboken, NJ: Wiley, pp. 113–14.

Matias, Cheryl E., and Colleen Boucher. 2023. "From Critical Whiteness Studies to a Critical Study of Whiteness: Restoring Criticality in Critical Whiteness Studies." *Whiteness and Education* 8(1):64–81.

May, Vivian M. 2015. *Pursuing Intersectionality, Unsettling Dominant Imaginaries*. New York: Routledge.

Mayne, Michael. 2019. "White Nationalism and the Rhetoric of Nostalgia." In *Affect, Emotion, and Rhetorical Persuasion in Mass Communication*, edited by L. Zhang and C. Clark. New York: Routledge, pp. 81–92.

Mihesuah, Devon A. 2000. "American Indian Identities: Issues of Individual Choice and Development." In *Contemporary Native American Cultural Issues*, edited by D. Champagne. Lanham, MD: AltaMira Press, pp. 13–38.

Miller, Paula K. 2022. "Hegemonic Whiteness: Expanding and Operationalizing the Conceptual Framework." *Sociology Compass*, e12973.

Mills, C. Wright. 1959. *The Sociological Imagination*. New York: Oxford University Press.

Miranda, Alexis R., Amaya Perez-Brumer, and Brittany M. Charlton. 2023. "Latino? Latinx? Latine? A Call for Inclusive Categories in Epidemiologic Research." *American Journal of Epidemiology* 192(12):1929–32.

Mohanty, Chandra Talpade. 1991. "Under Western Eyes: Feminist Scholarship and Colonial Discourses." In *Third World Women and the Politics of Feminism*, edited by C.T. Mohanty, A.

References

159

Russo, and L. Torres. Bloomington: Indiana University Press, pp. 51–80.

Monk Jr., Ellis P., Michael H. Esposito, and Hedwig Lee. 2021. "Beholding Inequality: Race, Gender, and Returns to Physical Attractiveness in the United States." *American Journal of Sociology* 127(1):194–241.

Moore, Mignon R. 2006. "Lipstick or Timberlands? Meanings of Gender Presentation in Black Lesbian Communities." *Signs: Journal of Women in Culture and Society* 32(1):113–39.

Moraga, Cherríe. 2015. "La Güera." In *This Bridge Called My Back: Writings by Radical Women of Color*. 4th edition. Edited by C. Moraga and G. Anzaldúa. Albany, NY: SUNY Press, pp. 22–9.

Morgensen, Scott Lauria. 2009. "Arrival at Home: Radical Faerie Configurations of Sexuality and Place." *GLQ: A Journal of Lesbian and Gay Studies* 15(1):67–96.

Morris, Edward W. 2005. "'Tuck in that Shirt!' Race, Class, Gender, and Discipline in an Urban School." *Sociological Perspectives* 48(1):25–48.

Mukhopadhyay, Carol C. 2008. "Getting Rid of the Word 'Caucasian.'" In *Everyday Antiracism: Getting Real About Race in School*, edited by M. Pollock. New York: The New Press, pp. 231–6.

Müller, Martin. 2020. "In Search of the Global East: Thinking between North and South." *Geopolitics* 25(3):734–55.

Nagel, Joane. 1996. *American Indian Ethnic Renewal: Red Power and the Resurgence of Identity and Culture*. New York: Oxford University Press.

Nagel, Joane. 2003. *Race, Ethnicity, and Sexuality: Intimate Intersections, Forbidden Frontiers*. New York: Oxford University Press.

Namaste, Viviane. 2000. *Invisible Lives: The Erasure of Transsexual and Transgendered People*. Chicago, IL: University of Chicago Press.

Noble, Bobby J. 2006. "Our Bodies are Not Ourselves: Tranny Guys and the Racialized Class Politics of Embodiment." In *Sons of the Movement: FtMs Risking Incoherence on a Post-Queer Cultural Landscape*. Toronto, Canada: Women's Press, pp. 76–100.

160   References

Nokes, Greg. n.d. "Black Exclusion Laws in Oregon." *Oregon Encyclopedia: A Project of the Oregon Historical Society,* www.oregonencyclopedia.org.

Omi, Michael, and Howard Winant. 1994. *Racial Formation in the United States: From the 1960s to the 1990s.* 2nd ed. New York: Routledge.

Pascoe, C. J. 2005. "'Dude, You're a Fag': Adolescent Masculinity and the Fag Discourse." *Sexualities* 8(3):329–46.

Peña, Susana. 2010. "Gender and Sexuality in Latina/o Miami: Documenting Latina Transsexual Activists." *Gender & History* 22(3):755–72.

Purdie-Vaughns, Valerie, and Richard P. Elbach. 2008. "Intersectional Invisibility: The Distinctive Advantages and Disadvantages of Multiple Subordinate-Group Identities." *Sex Roles* 59(5/6): 377–91.

Pyle, Kai. 2019. "'Women and 2spirits': On the Marginalization of Transgender Indigenous People in Activist Rhetoric." *American Indian Culture and Research Journal* 43(3):85–94.

Rahman, Momin. 2009. "Theorising Intersectionality: Identities, Equality and Ontology." In *Intersectionality and Beyond: Law, Power and the Politics of Location,* edited by E. Grabham, D. Cooper, J. Krishnadas, and D. Herman. New York: Routledge-Cavendish, pp. 352–73.

Rahman, Momin. 2010. "Queer as Intersectionality: Theorizing Gay Muslim Identities." *Sociology* 44(5):944–61.

Reay, Barry. 2020. *Trans America: A Counter-History.* Cambridge: Polity Press.

Reed, Kaitlin. 2023. "'We are a Part of the Land and the Land is Us': Settler Colonialism, Genocide, and Healing in California." In *Genocide and Mass Violence in the Age of Extremes,* edited by F. Jacob and M. Göllnitz. Berlin: De Gruyter, pp. 237–63.

Rifkin, Mark. 2012. *The Erotics of Sovereignty: Queer Native Writing in the Era of Self-Determination.* Minneapolis: University of Minnesota Press.

Risling Baldy, Cutcha. 2013. "Why We Gather: Traditional Gathering

References

in Native Northwest California and the Future of Bio-Cultural Sovereignty." *Ecological Processes* 2:1–10.

Rivera, Christopher. 2014. "The Brown Threat: Post-9/11 Conflations of Latina/os and Middle Eastern Muslims in the US American Imagination." *Latino Studies* 12(1):44–64.

Rizki, Cole. 2019. "Latin/x American Trans Studies: Toward a *Travesti*-Trans Analytic." *Transgender Studies Quarterly* 6(2):145–55.

Robinson, Margaret. 2020. "Two-Spirit Identity in a Time of Gender Fluidity." *Journal of Homosexuality* 67(12):1675–90.

Rodríguez, Clara E., ed. 1997. *Latin Looks: Images of Latinas and Latinos in the U.S. Media.* Boulder, CO: Westview Press.

Roen, Katrina. 2001. "Transgender Theory and Embodiment: The Risk of Racial Marginalisation." *Journal of Gender Studies* 10(3):253–63.

Rubin, Henry. 2003. *Self-Made Men: Identity and Embodiment Among Transsexual Men.* Nashville, TN: Vanderbilt University Press.

Sanday, Peggy Reeves. 1990. *Fraternity Gang Rape: Sex, Brotherhood and Privilege on Campus.* New York: New York University Press.

Schilt, Kristen. 2006. "Just One of the Guys?: How Transmen Make Gender Visible at Work." *Gender & Society* 20(4):465–90.

Schilt, Kristen, and Danya Lagos. 2017. "The Development of Transgender Studies in Sociology." *Annual Review of Sociology* 43(1):425–43.

Schippers, Mimi. 2007. "Recovering the Feminine Other: Masculinity, Femininity, and Gender Hegemony." *Theory and Society* 36:85–102.

Schweighofer, Katherine. 2018. "A Land of One's Own: Whiteness and Indigeneity on Lesbian Land." *Settler Colonial Studies* 8(4):489–506.

Sevelius, Jae M. 2013. "Gender Affirmation: A Framework for Conceptualizing Risk Behavior Among Transgender Women of Color." *Sex Roles* 68(11–12):675–89.

Shakespeare, Tom, Kath Gillespie-Sells, and Dominic Davies. 1996.

The Sexual Politics of Disability: Untold Desires. London: Cassell.

Siegel, Michael. 2020. "Racial Disparities in Fatal Police Shootings: An Empirical Analysis Informed by Critical Race Theory." *Boston University Law Review* 100:1069–92.

Sims, Jennifer Patrice. 2016. "Reevaluation of the Influence of Appearance and Reflected Appraisals for Mixed-Race Identity: The Role of Consistent Inconsistent Racial Perception." *Sociology of Race and Ethnicity* 2(4):569–83.

Smith, Dorothy E. 1990. "Women's Perspective as a Radical Critique of Sociology." *Sociological Inquiry* 44(1):7–13.

Smith-Johnson, Madeline. 2022. "Transgender Adults Have Higher Rates of Disability Than Their Cisgender Counterparts." *Health Affairs* 41(10):1470–6.

Snorton, C. Riley. 2017. *Black on Both Sides: A Racial History of Trans Identity*. Minneapolis: University of Minnesota Press.

Snow, David A., Louis A. Zurcher, and Gideon Sjoberg. 1982. "Interviewing by Comment: An Adjunct to the Direct Question." *Qualitative Sociology* 5(4):285–311.

Soto Vega, Karrieann, and Karma R. Chávez. 2018. "Latinx Rhetoric and Intersectionality in Racial Rhetorical Criticism." *Communication and Critical/Cultural Studies* 15(4):319–25.

Southern, Rosalynd, and Emily Harmer. 2019. "Othering Political Women: Online Misogyny, Racism and Ableism Towards Women in Public Life." In *Online Othering: Exploring Digital Violence and Discrimination on the Web*, edited by K. Lumsden and E. Harmer. Cham: Palgrave Macmillan, pp. 187–210.

Sowards, Stacey K. 2021. "Rhetoricity of Borders: Whiteness in Latinidad and Beyond." *Communication and Critical/Cultural Studies* 18(1):41–9.

Spade, Dean. 2015. *Normal Life: Administrative Violence, Critical Trans Politics, and the Limits of Law*. Durham, NC: Duke University Press.

SPLC (Southern Poverty Law Center). n.d. "In 2022, 24 Hate and Antigovernment Groups were Tracked in Oregon," https://www.splcenter.org/states/oregon.

References

Stanley, Eric A., and Nat Smith, eds. 2015. *Captive Genders: Trans Embodiment and the Prison Industrial Complex*. 2nd ed. Oakland, CA: AK Press.

Strauss, Anselm L. 1987. *Qualitative Analysis for Social Scientists*. New York: Cambridge University Press.

Strauss, Anselm, and Juliet Corbin. 1990. *Basics of Qualitative Research: Grounded Theory Procedures and Techniques*. Thousand Oaks, CA: Sage.

Sumerau, J. E., and Eric Anthony Grollman. 2020. *Black Lives and Bathrooms: Racial and Gendered Reactions to Minority Rights Movements*. Lanham, MD: Lexington Books.

Tatum, Beverly Daniel. 2003. *Why are All the Black Kids Sitting Together in the Cafeteria?: And Other Conversations about Race*. Rev. ed. New York: Basic Books.

Taylor, Yvette, Sally Hines, and Mark E. Casey, eds. 2010. *Theorizing Intersectionality and Sexuality*. New York: Palgrave Macmillan.

Thai, Jayden L., Stephanie L. Budge, and Laurie D. McCubbin. 2021. "Qualitative Examination of Transgender Asian Americans Navigating and Negotiating Cultural Identities and Values." *Asian American Journal of Psychology* 12(4):301–16.

Tinsley, Omise'eke Natasha, and Matt Richardson. 2014. "From Black Transgender Studies to Colin Dayan: Notes on Methodology." *Small Axe: A Caribbean Journal of Criticism* 18(3):152–61.

Torkelson, Jason, and Douglas Hartmann. 2020. "The Racialization of Ethnicity: The New Face of White Ethnicity in Postmillennial America." *Sociology of Race and Ethnicity* 6(3):302–18.

Turban, Jack L., Katherine L. Kraschel, and I. Glenn Cohen. 2021. "Legislation to Criminalize Gender-Affirming Medical Care for Transgender Youth." *JAMA* 325(22):2251–2.

Valentine, David. 2007. *Imagining Transgender: An Ethnography of a Category*. Durham, NC: Duke University Press.

Vargas, Deborah R. 2010. "Representations of Latina/o Sexuality in Popular Culture." In *Latina/o Sexualities: Probing Powers, Passions, Practices, and Policies*, edited by M. Asencio. New Brunswick, NJ: Rutgers University Press, pp. 117–36.

Vargas, Nicholas, and Jared Kingsbury. 2016. "Racial Identity Contestation: Mapping and Measuring Racial Boundaries." *Sociology Compass* 10(8):718–29.

Vasquez, Jessica M. 2010. "Blurred Borders for Some But Not 'Others': Racialization, 'Flexible Ethnicity,' Gender, and Third-generation Mexican American Identity." *Sociological Perspectives* 53(1):45–71.

Vasquez-Tokos, Jessica. 2020. "Do Latinos Consider Themselves Mainstream? The Influence of Region." *Sociological Perspectives* 63(4):571–88.

Verloo, Mieke. 2006. "Multiple Inequalities, Intersectionality and the European Union." *European Journal of Women's Studies* 13(3):211–28.

Vidal-Ortiz, Salvador. 2009. "The Figure of the Transwoman of Color Through the Lens of 'Doing Gender.'" *Gender & Society* 23(1):99–103.

Walker, Ruth V., Sara M. Powers, and Tarynn M. Witten. 2023. "Transgender and Gender Diverse People's Fear of Seeking and Receiving Care in Later Life: A Multiple Method Analysis." *Journal of Homosexuality* 70(14):3374–98.

Walton, Jessica, and Mandy Truong. 2023. "A Review of the Model Minority Myth: Understanding the Social, Educational and Health Impacts." *Ethnic and Racial Studies* 46(3):391–419.

Ward, Jane. 2008. "White Normativity: The Cultural Dimensions of Whiteness in a Racially Diverse LGBT Organization." *Sociological Perspectives* 51(3):563–86.

Warner, David F., and Tyson H. Brown. 2011. "Understanding How Race/Ethnicity and Gender Define Age-Trajectories of Disability: An Intersectionality Approach." *Social Science & Medicine* 72(8):1236–48.

Wentling, Tre. 2020. "Contested Citizenship: Renaming Processes Among People of Transgender Experience." *Journal of Homosexuality* 67(12):1653–74.

West, Candace, and Don H. Zimmerman. 1987. "Doing Gender." *Gender & Society* 1(2):125–51.

Weston, Kathleen. 2004. "Fieldwork in Lesbian and Gay

References

Communities." In *Approaches to Qualitative Research: A Reader on Theory and Practice*, edited by S. N. Hesse-Biber and P. Leavy. New York: Oxford University Press, pp. 177–84.

White, Francis Ray. 2014. "Fat/Trans: Queering the Activist Body." *Fat Studies* 3(2):86–100.

Wilkins, Amy C. 2004. "Puerto Rican Wannabes: Sexual Spectacle and the Making of Race, Class, and Gender Boundaries." *Gender & Society* 18(1):103–21.

Wu, Ellen D. 2014. *The Color of Success: Asian Americans and the Origins of the Model Minority*. Princeton, NJ: Princeton University Press.

Yarbro-Bejarano, Yvonne. 1999. "Sexuality and Chicana/o Studies: Toward a Theoretical Paradigm for the Twenty-First Century." *Cultural Studies* 13(2):335–45.

Yuval-Davis, Nira. 1997. *Gender and Nation*. Thousand Oaks, CA: Sage.

Yuval-Davis, Nira. 2006. "Intersectionality and Feminist Politics." *European Journal of Women's Studies* 13(3):193–209.

Zabus, Chantel, and David Coad, eds. 2014. *Transgender Experience: Place, Ethnicity, and Visibility*. New York: Routledge.

Zamantakis, Alithia. 2022. "Queering Intimate Emotions: Trans/Nonbinary People Negotiating Emotional Expectations in Intimate Relationships." *Sexualities* 25(5–6):581–97.

Zinn, Maxine Baca, and Bonnie Thornton Dill. 1996. "Theorizing Difference from Multiracial Feminism." *Feminist Studies* 22(2):321–31.

Index

Abelson, Miriam J. 39, 77, 96
ability, in intersectional model 8–9,
  17, 22–3, 26, 29
  see also disability; ableism
ableism 22–3
activism 6–7, 32–3
  calls to action 120–1, 133–8
aesthetic capital 24–5
African American *see* Black trans
  people
age, in intersectional model 8–9,
  17, 22
Ahmed, Sara 77, 80, 145
Aizura, Aren Z. 115
Alimahomed, Sabrina 86
alloism 21
Anthias, Floya 7, 10, 26–7
antiracism 74, 85
Anzaldúa, Gloria 45, 65, 69
Asian American trans people
  community 34
  experiences of intersectionality
    67–8, 117–21
  experiences with whiteness 81–2,
    86
  familial expectations 34, 86
  hypersexualization 41, 44–5,
    102–4

social visibility 42–3, 44–5, 122
surveillance 122–3
transitioning 43
workplace experiences 41,
  117–18
Azhar, Sameena 44

Baklâ 67
Bilge, Sirma 6–7
Black trans people
  and disability 110–11
  exclusion of 32–3
  experiences with whiteness
    80–1
  hypersexualization/
    desexualization 107–10
  sexuality 107–9
  social visibility 43–4
  status in Black community 35, 36,
    37–8
  stigmatization of 46, 47–49
  surveillance 122
  workplace experiences 39–41
body size, in intersectional model
  8–9, 17, 24
borderlands 55, 65, 69
Boucher, Colleen 79
Brekhus, Wayne 10

Index

brown threat 63
Brumbaugh-Johnson, Stacey M. 128–9

caste 25
Chávez, Karma R. 61, 62
Chavis, Ben 19
Chou, Rosalind S. 42–3
cisgenderism 18–19, 85
citizenship 60, 112–16
  see also nationality
Clare, Eli 26
class *see* social class
classism 22
  in intersection 6, 99
Collins, Patricia Hill 5, 6–7, 7, 11, 45, 46
colorism 61, 68
Combahee River Collective 6
community building 135–8
Connell, Raewyn 38
Cooley, Charles Horton 57
Crenshaw, Kimberlé 6
criminal justice system 47–51
  police officers 48–9
  policing 47–9
critical mixed-race studies (CMRS) 56–7
critical whiteness studies
  and trans studies 76–80
Cromwell, Jason 39
culture, in intersectional model 8–9, 17, 20–1
cultural capital 20

Daniel, G. Reginald 56–7
desexualization 44, 102–3, 107–10
disability
  in intersectional model 8–9, 17, 22–3, 26, 29
  trans BIPOC experiences 29, 109–10, 110–12
documentation
  driver's licenses 48–9, 114
  green cards 113–14
  gun licenses 114–15

Dozier, Raine 39
drag kings 107–8

employment 39–41, 100, 101–2, 117–18
  see also workplace experiences
Espiritu, Yen Le 20
ethnicity, in intersectional model 8–9, 17, 20
ethnocentrism 20

Feagin, Joe R. 42–3
femininities, hierarchy of 38
feminist standpoint theory 7, 11

gender, in intersectional model 8–10, 17, 18–19, 27–9
gendered racialization 32–53
  racialization, use of term 18
  racial and ethnic expectations 33–8
  hypervisibility and invisibility 42–51
  and white settler supremacy 38–42
gendered spaces 32–3, 35–6, 38
Global East 23
Gonzales, Gabrielle G. 62
Gundemeda, Nagaraju 25

Hamer, Katarzyna 20
Han, Chong-suk 43
Haraway, Donna 7
Hartmann, Douglas 78, 79, 88
health care access 101, 102
hegemony 15, 26, 41, 47, 56, 64, 65
  hegemonic gender 19, 38
  hegemonic sexuality 21
  hegemonic whiteness 10, 11
heterosexism 21
Holla, Sylvia 25
Holm, Tom J. 19
hooks, bell 132
Howard, Judith A. 13
Hsu, V. Jo 34
Hull, Kathleen E. 128–9

Index

hypersexualization 41, 43–6, 102–4, 107–8

immigration 113–14
Indigeneity, in intersectional model 8–9, 17, 19–20, 27
   see also Native American people; peoplehood matrix; Two-Spirit
interracial relationships 45, 85–6, 105–10
intersectional model
   categories 8–9, 16–24
   fluidity and transparency 24–7, 29–30
   intersectional prism 17
intersectional trans scholarship 14–16
intersectionality, definitions and use of term 5, 6–8

Jesperson, Jamey 84, 95–6, 101–2
Joshi, Khyati Y. 23–4

Khanna, Nikki 57
Kingsbury, Jared 68
Kuipers, Giselinde 25

Lagos, Danya 14
land ownership 93–4
land projects 94–6, 130–1
Latino/a/x/e 37
Latino/a/x/e trans people
   experiences with whiteness 82–5
   hypersexualization 45–6, 63, 69
   identity document changes 113–14
   other's perceptions of race 54–5, 59–64, 66–70
   status in Latinx community 36–7
   stigmatization of 47, 63
   workplace experiences 50–1
Lewis, Amanda E. 52
Lipsitz, George 79, 90
Lutz, Helma 8–9, 9

Manalansan, Martin F. 67
masculinities, hierarchy of 38
Matias, Cheryl E. 79
May, Vivian M. 7–8
McKay, Dwanna L. 19
middle class 22, 35, 43, 100–1, 115–16
   see also social class
Miller, Paula K. 10
monosexism 21
Moraga, Cherríe 65
Morgensen, Scott Lauria 94, 96
Morris, Edward W. 51
Mukhopadhyay, Carol C. 73
Müller, Martin 23
multiraciality 54–72
   intersectional approaches 56–8
   shifts in perception of others 59–70
   implications 71–2
multiracial trans people
   experiences of disability 111–12
   experiences with whiteness 84–5
   hypersexualization 45–6, 63, 69
   other's perceptions of race 1, 2, 4, 28, 54–5, 59–70
   transition 67–9
   see also multiraciality

Nagel, Joane 20, 45
nationalism 23, 85
nationality
   in intersectional model 8–9, 17, 23
   trans BIPOC experiences 112–16
Native American trans people
   Native identity 1–2, 3
   other's perceptions of race 1, 2, 4, 28, 64–6, 69–70, 107–8
   stigmatization of 46
   see also Two-Spirit
Noble, Bobby J. 77–8

Omi, Michael 56

Index

panethnicity 20
parents' experiences 104, 123
participants
  Alejandro 47
  Amber 22, 34, 41, 44, 103–4, 117–21, 122, 123, 133, 136
  April 73–6, 97
  Aria 123–5
  Ata 88
  Aurora 88–90
  Bazil 107–8
  Bennyboy 38–9, 67–8
  Brandon 129–30
  Chance 108–9
  Charlie 92–3, 126–8
  Craig 87
  D 126
  Dante 43, 81–2, 86, 122–3, 123, 137
  Dexter 36, 45–6, 67, 68–9, 107, 110
  Diego 36, 54–5, 59–62, 63–4
  Elle 43, 103, 136–7
  Jacobo 36, 37, 50–1, 137–8
  Jake 21–2, 36, 40–1, 46, 52
  Janice 37–8
  Joe 99, 110–11, 135
  Josie 32–3, 35, 38, 52, 101
  Katrice 32–3, 38, 52
  Kitty 125–6
  Lance 1–4, 27–30, 46, 59, 64–6, 99–100, 133–5, 136, 138
  Lee 87
  Leela 85–6
  Lola 37–8
  Lucas 91–2, 95–6, 131
  Marisol 82–4, 113–14
  Miranda 41, 45
  Morgan 69–70
  Nici 41, 44
  Paige 105–7
  Rebecca 105, 107
  Scout 45, 59, 62–4, 84–5, 109–10, 111–12, 121
  Sky 130
  Steve 47–9, 80–1, 122, 123
  Switch 131–3
  Topher 104, 123
  Trent 39–40, 46
  Valentina 135–6
partners of trans people 37–8, 85–6, 105–7, 108–9
Pearson, Diane 19
peoplehood matrix 19
poverty rates 100
  see also social class
power structures, relevance of 10–11

race
  centrality to trans liberation 32–3
  in intersectional model 8–10, 17, 18, 27–9
  see also gendered racialization; multiraciality; whiteness
racial identity contestation 67–8
racial victimhood 76
racism 18, 66, 76, 77, 78, 83–4, 87, 89, 96, 105, 119
  in intersection 6, 19, 40, 94
  see also antiracism
reflected appraisals framework 57–8
religion
  in intersectional model 8–9, 17, 23–4
  Christian normativity 23–4
  paganism 88
Renfrow, Daniel G. 13
research methodology 139–45
Rivera, Christopher 63
Rubin, Henry 39
rural trans people 77, 94–6, 130–1

Schilt, Kristen 14, 39, 45
settler colonialism 19, 27, 44, 93–6
settler transnationalism 84
settler white supremacy *see* whiteness
sexism 18, 38–9
  in intersection 6, 19
sexuality
  in intersectional model 8–10, 17, 21–2

sexuality (*cont.*)
   trans BIPOC experiences 21–2,
     102–10
   see also desexualization;
     heterosexism;
     hypersexualization; interracial
     relationships; monosexism
Sims, Jennifer Patrice 60
sizeism 24
Smith-Johnson, Madeline 110
social attractiveness 24–5
social change 100, 128, 130,132–3,
   135–5
social class
   in intersectional model 8–10, 17,
     22, 29
   trans experiences 29, 40–1, 43,
     50–1, 98–102
   see also classism; middle class;
     poverty rates; working class
social structures, relevance of 10–11
social visibility 42–51
Soto Vega, Karrieann 61, 62
Sowards, Stacey K. 84
Spade, Dean 113
surveillance 47–8, 80–1, 122–3,
   130–1
symbolic interactionism 12–14

Tatum, Beverly Daniel 89–90
Thai, Jayden L. 34
Torkelson, Jason 78, 79, 88
trans support groups 32–3, 74
Truong, Mandy 82
Two-Spirit 3–4

unemployment rate 100
US Transgender Survey 100

Vargas, Nicholas 68
Vasquez, Jessica M. 61

Walton, Jessica 82
Ward, Jane 28, 52

Wentling, Tre 112
West, Candace 12, 19
White, Francis Ray 24
whiteness 73–97
   category of 10–11, 77, 79
   Caucasian 73–4
   parents and assimilation 1–3,
     68
   and settler colonialism 44, 93–6
   trans BIPOC experiences 27–8,
     32–3, 38–42, 80–6
   views on social class 101
   white habitus 78–9
   white normativity 28
   white trans people's approaches
     73–6, 77–9, 86–93
white trans people
   approaches to politics 123–8,
     129–33
   approaches to whiteness 73–6,
     88–90, 91–3
   class status 101
   driver's/gun licenses 114–15
   land project experiences 95–6,
     130–1
   see also whiteness

Winant, Howard 56
working class
   approaches to whiteness 87, 91–2,
     96
   building solidarity 99–100
   cultural capital 29
   poverty and access to resources
     100–1
   sexuality 107–10
   stigmatization of 46–7
   use of term 22
   workplace experiences 50–1
   see also social class
workplace experiences 39–41, 50–1,
   117–18, 122–3

Zimmerman, Don H. 12, 19